Literacy in Action: Football

Get ready for kick off and prepare to meet all of your literacy goals with *Literacy in Action: Football.*

All Year 5 and particularly Year 6 teachers know about the pressure to help children deliver levels of achievement laid down by higher authorities than themselves. Many of the reluctant writers are passionate about football. *Literacy in Action: Football* could be the answer to their and your prayers, offering expert, tried and trusted techniques for teaching literacy, developed within the context of the "Beautiful Game." For those not bitten by the football bug there are alternative options. *Literacy in Action: Football* is a fun and inspiring addition to your literacy teaching.

This unique classroom resource contains twenty-four lesson plans, each structured like a football match. For an hour, transform your classroom into Wembley Stadium! Each detailed lesson plan includes:

- Short, kinaesthetic, focused tasks with instant feedback and praise
- Speaking and listening exercises – children engage in talking and collaborative work before completing a writing task
- Special notes for teachers summarising key points from research into boy's writing
- Alternative tasks available for those not interested in football
- Differentiated material for a wide ability range

Literacy in Action: Football is written by Heather Butler, a writer, literacy consultant and story writing workshop leader. *Literacy in Action: Football* has been tested extensively by Year 5 and Year 6 teachers in leafy-green, inner city, multi-cultural and rural settings with amazing results. Why not try it for yourself?

Literacy in Action: Football

24 Flexible Lessons for Ages 9–11

By Heather Butler

Routledge
Taylor & Francis Group

LONDON AND NEW YORK

First edition published 2010
by Routledge
2 Park Square, Milton Park, Abingdon, Oxon OX14 4RN

Simultaneously published in the USA and Canada
by Routledge
270 Madison Avenue, New York, NY 10016

Routledge is an imprint of the Taylor & Francis Group, an informa business

© 2010 Heather Butler
Typeset in Galliard by
Keystroke, Tettenhall, Wolverhampton
Printed and bound in Great Britain by
TJ International Ltd, Padstow, Cornwall

British Library Cataloguing in Publication Data
A catalogue record for this book is available from the British Library

Library of Congress Cataloging-in-Publication Data
Butler, Heather.
Literacy in action : football : 24 flexible lessons for ages 9–11 / by Heather Butler. – 1st ed.
p. cm.
Includes bibliographical references.
1. Language arts (Elementary)–Activity programs–Great Britain. 2. Language arts–Correlation with
content subjects–Great Britain. 3. Soccer–Great Britain. I. Title.
LB1576.B965 2010
372.6'044–dc22
2009049782

ISBN10: 0–415–56486–7 (hbk)
ISBN10: 0–415–56485–9 (pbk)
ISBN10: 0–203–85029–7 (ebk)

ISBN13: 978–0–415–56486–1 (hbk)
ISBN13: 978–0–415–56485–4 (pbk)
ISBN13: 978–0–203–85029–9 (ebk)

Contents

About the book

At Manor Farm Community Junior School, children would arrive in upper KS2 with writing abilities ranging from levels 1 to 5. These, inevitably, included a group of boys who thought of little else but football. They actually reached the national schools football finals when they were in year 6. Their talent for reaching literacy level 4 seemed less sparkling, so a series of lessons was created to tap into their testosterone-fuelled imaginations.

Each contained short, often **kinaesthetic, targeted activities** taught as a football match. **Differentiation** was four-way:

- level 2
- low and secure level 3
- high level 3/low level 4c
- secure and high level 4/level 5

Content covered a variety of writing skills. If appropriate, children could focus on just one of those (e.g. with a teaching assistant) while the lesson continued for everyone else.

Revision of previous learning was often included, based on the premise that some children did not absorb learning the first time round.

Lessons were officially **an hour long** (though some needed a little longer) and, apart from three story-writing ones, were completely **stand alone**. They could be taught as a week's input or as one-offs, and not necessarily in published sequence.

Raising self-esteem by **self-assessing** and highlighting *I CAN . . .* **targets** was an integral option for all lessons. Children were to **achieve and feel good** about their writing. Consequently, *I CAN . . .* targets do not cover every aspect needed to formally achieve a level. They are user-friendly, easily assessed, "we can do this" targets.

What about children who didn't "do" football?

Most lessons had two strands, football and non-football. Wherever possible, the reference was to "sport" rather than "football." Children were given as much choice as possible in terms of what they wrote about.

Who wrote and piloted the lessons?

Heather Butler teaches two days a week at Manor Farm Community Junior School in Hazlemere, Bucks. She also writes children's books and education resource material and runs inset and whole-school story-writing workshops across the UK. With over twenty-five years in UK classrooms behind her, she is passionate about children achieving high quality writing. She created and wrote the lessons. For more details go to: www.heatherbutler.info.

Angela Bray, senior teacher at Manor Farm Community Junior School in Hazlemere, Bucks has taught for over twenty years. She has mentored teachers-in-training and as English subject leader introduced a series of initiatives to raise writing standards. She, along with **David Edwards**, helped make the lessons happen.

After their first outing and evaluation, lessons were sent to other schools for further comment. Thank you to **Mary Harris** (Leamore, Walsall), **Peter Williams** (Altham St James C of E Primary, Lancs), **Parmjit Rava** and **Sukhdeep Shetia** (Blair Peach Primary, Southall, London) and **Sarah Butler** (Robertswood Junior School, Chalfont St Peter, Bucks). Thanks also to **Kai Jones**, and **Harriet and Rosalind Firth** who helped with the artwork.

Writing's all right

level 2	Paperclip Premiers (PPs)
level 3c/3b	Chosen Champs (CCs)
level 3a/4c	Dream Division (DD)
level 4b/4a+	Longstop Leaguers (LLs)

Game plan

Children will: sign contracts, sort out *I CAN . . .* writing target sheets and write about themselves as writers.

Training

For children

None.

For teachers (preparation for the lesson)

1 Photocopy the correct *target sheet* for each child – see pages 144–153. The levels on these are shown in the top right-hand corner; 3 – – is low level 3; – 3 – is secure level 3; – – 3 is high level 3. These are key targets for the level. They do not constitute the complete skillset needed to achieve a level but have been chosen because they are child friendly for self-assessment purposes. Paperclip Premiers (PPs) are children working at level 2; Chosen Champs (CCs) are working at low and secure level 3; Dream Division (DD) are working at high level 3 and low level 4; and Longstop Leaguers (LLs) are working at secure and high level 4 and level 5.

2 Eco-copy and chop *We want to be part of this project because . . .* , one for each child, as found on page 4. The term eco-copy is used when items for children are duplicated on a page to reduce photocopying.

3 Photocopy and chop *"Writing's all right," said Mr Wright / Report Writing* on page 5 – one per child.

4 Photocopy several *Report writing* sheets as found on page 6 for those who might need it.

The match

Warm-up (often revision of previously learned skills)

- **Introduce the idea of football–related literacy lessons** and stress that, wherever possible, children will be given a choice between writing about football or an alternative. They can choose each lesson. They will be asked to work collaboratively, just as real writers often work together. Tasks will be short and achievable, hopefully completed within a one-hour time limit. Children will evaluate their own writing, often with a partner, and work out what they have learned during the process. *I CAN . . .* target sheets will help them to do this.
- **Give out** *We want to be part of this project because . . .* and ask children to sign and decorate them. Give time to practise "official" signatures.
- Stick these in the front of their books.
- Also give out the appropriate *I CAN . . .* **writing target** sheet to each child. These need to be stuck in the back of their books.

First half (develops the WARM-UP or introduces the lesson's theme)

- Hand out *"Writing's all right," said Mr Wright* and read through each item. Ask children to write a number to show how they would feel if asked to do it: 1 is the lowest (least enthusiastic), 10 is the highest (most enthusiastic).
- Stick these in the front of books and ask children to compare their ratings with a partner, saying why they would or would not enjoy writing each.

Half-time (Particularly Energetic Participation talk has children moving around)

- Ask children to stand behind their chairs and **dance energetically** several times while **rapping** *"I like school, I like school. The students and teachers are really cool."*
- Challenge children to think of something better. The PEP talk will be a weekly feature for them to devise their own raps (vetted by an adult) and lead this part of the lesson.

Second half (the focused writing bit)

- Talk about **vocabulary and phrases teachers use** when they write reports.
- Make a list of these on the board, such as:

  - He/she is good at . . .
  - Their greatest achievement has been . . .
  - It has been a pleasure to see that he/she can now . . .
  - He/she has so enjoyed . . .
  - He/she has become more accurate . . .
  - He/she has tried really hard . . .
  - Presentation is now much . . .
  - Next year he/she needs to improve . . .

- Ask children to **write a report about themselves as writers**. *Report Writing* will help children who are unsure what to focus on. Allow Paperclips to write on their sheet while everyone else writes prose in their books.

Extra time *(for early finishers, possible homework ideas and suggestions to make this lesson extend to two lessons)*

Ask children to write a report about themselves for other curriculum areas.

Write a report on an author, critiquing the style and content of a chosen book.

The analysis (plenary)

Ask children to **share their report with a friend**.

Shoot-out *(target highlighting. Recommended use once every 3–4 weeks)*

These are to encourage children, provide a further writing focus and contribute towards self-assessment.

Further explanation and specific *I CAN . . .* targets are given in lesson 2.

FOOTBALL BUBBLE

Boys find doing anything AND listening harder than girls do. Give instructions and teaching when fingers are still and eyes focused on the speaker.

We want to be part of this project because...

1   It will help us become better writers.

2   We will be able to see how clever we are.

3   We like having a choice about what we write.

4   We like working with other children.

5   Completing a whole task in a lesson feels good.

6   Our teachers have promised to make it dead good.

Signed_____

We want to be part of this project because...

1   It will help us become better writers.

2   We will be able to see how clever we are.

3   We like having a choice about what we write.

4   We like working with other children.

5   Completing a whole task in a lesson feels good.

6   Our teachers have promised to make it dead good.

Signed_____

"Writing's all right," said Mr Wright

How would you feel if you were asked to . . .

1	Write about something you like.	
2	Write a story.	
3	Eat a plate of your favourite food.	
4	Write an email.	
5	Go home at the end of the day.	
6	Laugh at a teacher's joke when it's not really funny.	
7	Write a diary about what you did yesterday.	
8	Create a character to write about.	
9	Spell a difficult word.	
10	Reread and edit something you have just finished writing.	
11	Draw something before you write about it.	
12	Work really fast because you will only be working on that task for a few minutes.	
13	Know why you are writing something down.	
14	Talk about your ideas before you start writing.	

Report writing

■ Where your ideas come from

■ Playing with words in your head

■ Editing

■ Commenting about others' writing

■ Handwriting

■ Good books you've read

■ Spelling

■ Which part of writing you would like to be better at

■ Your preference – writing stories or writing non-fiction

■ What you get confused about (like paragraphs, speech marks, sentences, connectives)

"Writing Rocks" quiz show

level 2	Paperclip Premiers (PPs)
level 3c/3b	Chosen Champs (CCs)
level 3a/4c	Dream Division (DD)
level 4b/4a+	Longstop Leaguers (LLs)

Game plan

Children will: use technical vocabulary, question marks and non-fiction texts for research, then take part in a quiz.

Training

For children

Bring non-fiction books about anything they are interested in – including football.

For teachers

1 Have a supply of non-fiction books ready for children who forget.
2 Eco-copy and chop "*Writing Rocks*" quiz scaffolds on pages 10 and 11.
3 Dig out some props for Quibble the Question Master to wear.
4 Put children into writing ability groups.

The match

Warm-up

- Let children know **which league** they are in and sit them in their groups.
- Introduce the term "**technical words**." These are words which are specific to a generic subject. So words associated with "car" are gears, vehicle, steering wheel, axle.
- Ask children to work with a partner to think of technical words to go with "football," "swimming" or another "current" word. On the board write the key word (e.g. "football") in the middle and related words round it.
- Share good words children have thought of.

First half

- The TV quiz programme **Writing Rocks** is being recorded next week. Using non-fiction books, the Internet or other sources, children are to contribute questions and answers for the quiz and also record answers and page numbers showing where the information was found.
- Model how to write **interesting questions** that do not have yes/no or one-word answers, remind children to use **question marks** and show children how to write **good answers**.
- All **technical words** are to be underlined or written in colour.
- Hand out **Writing Rocks** quiz slips so that children know what is expected of them.

Half-time PEP talk

- **Stand and chant** the following in army route-march style while jogging on the spot:

  Quest-i-ons need question marks,
  Yes no answers are not smart, Tech-ni-cal words should be used,
  They are written by cool dudes.

- Remind children that they can lead this part of the lesson if they can invent a suitable rhyme to chant about any area of literacy.

Second half

Complete **quiz questions** and check that technical words have been underlined and question marks used. Ask children to choose their favourite question.

Extra time

- Ask children to make spider diagrams with a generic word in the middle and technical words radiating out of it.
- Ask children to write a full script for a quiz radio programme, researching questions and using question marks.

The analysis

Now **hold the quiz** with Quibble the Question Master as the presenter. Dress a child up to be Quibble. Ask the child to come to the front of the classroom and read out his or her favourite question. Give everyone 5 seconds to pair-share possible answers. Quibble then chooses who will answer. If he is a boy, he must choose a girl and vice versa. Ask children to identify technical words used in the questions.

Shoot-out

I CAN . . . targets children might have met:

Low 2 (2 children): 7.

Low 3 (trainer): 4, 6.

Secure 3 (twirly flower): 10c.

High 3 (a cup of tea): 3c.

Low 4 (man crawling out of a shark's mouth): 4, 5.

Secure 4 (tiger saying "hello"): 4d, 6, 12.

High 4 (a bridge with a spider scurrying across it): 4.

Low 5 (Nigel the gnome): 8.

Ask children to highlight what they have achieved on the *I CAN* . . . sheet at the front of their books and write the date next to it. Then highlight the evidence for their achievement and write the *I CAN* . . . number in the margin. This makes gathering evidence for assessment very easy.

FOOTBALL BUBBLE

The skill of asking questions after looking at text is important. Adults find out about events by reading adverts and asking questions to clarify and plan.

"Writing Rocks" quiz

PPs

Use your non-fiction books to find questions and answers for the quiz.

Question . . .	Answer . . .	Page number

Question . . .	Answer . . .	Page number

© Heather Butler 2010 *Literacy in Action: Football* Routledge

"Writing Rocks" quiz

CCs

- Use your non-fiction books to find questions and answers for the quiz.

- Write questions (don't forget the ?) and the page numbers where you found the information you have used.

- Each answer needs to make a full, interesting sentence.

- Underline all technical words.

"Writing Rocks" quiz

DDs

- Use your non-fiction books to find questions and answers for the quiz.

- Write questions (don't forget the ?), the page numbers where you found the information and the name of the book you have used.

- Each answer needs to be written using two full and interesting sentences.

- Underline all technical words.

"Writing Rocks" quiz

LLs

- Use your non-fiction books to find questions and answers for the quiz.

- Write questions, the page numbers where you found the information and the name of the book you have used.

- Your answers need to be written using three or four full and interesting sentences.

- Underline all technical words.

Character profile

level 2	Paperclip Premiers (PPs)
level 3c/3b	Chosen Champs (CCs)
level 3a/4c	Dream Division (DD)
level 4b/4a+	Longstop Leaguers (LLs)

Game plan

Children will: identify and use good adjectives, similes and metaphors to write a character description of a famous person.

Training

For children

Bring in pictures of characters that can be stuck in their writing books (i.e. loose pages that can be cut out).

For teachers

1 Eco-copy the *Adjectives to describe players* on page 15 – enough for children to work in pairs or small groups. Cut the words up and put them in envelopes. Do not use more difficult words (i.e. right-hand column) for CCs and PPs.
2 Download a picture of a famous person ready to use on the interactive whiteboard.

The match

Warm-up

- Recap **adjectives, similes and metaphors**.
- Looking at pictures children have brought in, ask them to write down adjectives, similes and metaphors to describe what their characters **look** like – e.g. the muscle machine, like a frightened rabbit he tapped the ball.
- Expect DDs and LLs to write metaphors, CCs to write similes and PPs to use adjectives.
- Share several children's ideas and write them on the right-hand side of the board.

First half

- Give out the envelopes with *Adjectives to describe players* inside.
- Show a picture of a famous person on the interactive whiteboard and ask children to describe him or her by **taking slips of paper** out of the envelopes one at a time.
- This gives them **character traits**. Children are allowed to make up details about their characters.
- Working in pairs or small groups, using white boards, children should write two sentences about **when** their character might show this character trait. DDs and LLs should also write about **how** the character might show it.

    For example:

    - *Peter is very laid back when he is at home.* (DDs and LLs add . . .) *He wears his slippers even when being interviewed by the press.*
    - *Chloë is indecisive when it comes to buying clothes.* (DDs and LLs add . . .) *She spends hours just looking round the shops before buying anything.*

- Ask one or two children for their favourite sentences and write them on the left-hand side of the board.
- Tell children not to clean their whiteboards.

Half-time PEP talk

- Invite children to **pair up** the phrases on the board (or use other phrases not shared with the whole class and/or make up further new ones) to create two-line rhyming poems. Set a time limit (such as 2 minutes) then share what children have come up with and choose the best one.
- Ask everyone to stand up and act out the rhyme. For example:

    On the pitch he's an optimist with mean, keen eyes,
    He aims the ball and the keeper dives . . .

Second half

- Working on their own, ask children to **stick their own pictures** in their books. Glue will be tacky so tell children not to write over the picture but to write a physical description (using adjectives, similes and metaphors) to the right of the picture, and to write what the person is like inside – i.e. character traits – on the left-hand side.
- Give children 5 minutes to work in silence to **write a one-paragraph description** of their character using the words and phrases round their picture as if they were notes.

Extra time

Ask children to make a class list of similes and metaphors that are really useful for describing people and places, then write a description using prose.

The analysis

Swap books with a partner and take out two coloured pencils. Each child should find two things they really like about their friend's writing and underline it in one of the colours. They should then find one thing to improve and write the improvement in the other colour, in the margin or over the top if there is room.

Shoot-out

Specific targets for children to check and highlight are . . .

Low 2 (funny face): 7

Secure 2 (2 children): 4

High 2 (penguin on holiday): 1

Secure 3 (twirly flower): 5

High 3 (cup of tea): 4

FOOTBALL BUBBLE

Putting tasks in envelopes takes time but is a great way to differentiate discreetly and also to make children feel special.

Adjectives to describe players

team player	reserved
cheerful	ambitious
hard worker	trustworthy
impatient	optimistic
moody	sensitive
lazy	indecisive
laid back	sociable

Adjectives to describe players

team player	reserved
cheerful	ambitious
hard worker	trustworthy
impatient	optimistic
moody	sensitive
lazy	indecisive
laid back	sociable

Q&A conversations

level 2	Paperclip Premiers (PPs)
level 3c/3b	Chosen Champs (CCs)
level 3a/4c	Dream Division (DD)
level 4b/4a+	Longstop Leaguers (LLs)

Game plan

Children will: revisit conventions of speech, use adverbs and synonyms for "said" effectively and write a question and answer conversation between two imaginary characters going to a sports event.

Training

For children

None.

For teachers

1 Find props that identify someone going to a sports event.
2 Eco-copy and chop *Writing speech*, one between two, as found on pages 19 and 20.

The match

Using a different colour for punctuation write on the board **before children come into the classroom** in very large letters:

> *"The game's about to start," said Dad excitedly.*
> *"Who's going to win?" asked Mum enthusiastically.*

Warm-up

▪ Ask children to **invent actions** for each piece of punctuation OR use:

▪ Both hands make stars to the left and say "wheeee!" for opening speech marks.
▪ Both hands make stars to the right and say "wheeee!" to close speech marks.
▪ Touch the floor in a sweeping motion and say "uh-huh" for a comma.

- Call out "oink!" for a full stop and wave right hand.
- Make a squeaky noise for an apostrophe.
- Draw a large question mark in the air and make a loud sigh for a question mark.

- Read the sentences on the board with **participating punctuation** and recap how speech marks and commas work.

First half

- Dress a child in the sports event props; he or she is travelling to a match. Hot-seat the child, modelling suitable questions and drawing out full answers.
- In pairs, ask children to **think of questions** they might ask this person and check that they are sensible questions.
- In their books ask children to write their best question down – who said it and how.
- Now put speech marks round the question part of the sentence.
- While children are busy, write sentences for HALF-TIME PEP TALK on the board.

Half-time PEP talk

Read the sentences in participating punctuation style after creating a sign for exclamation marks. For example:

"The ref's wrong!" the crowd screamed angrily.
Ahmed sighed sadly and whispered, "they've lost again."

Second half

In their books, ask children to **write a conversation between two characters**, using correct punctuation, interesting verbs (i.e. synonyms for said) and adverbs. Both characters need names. They do not have to be excited about where they are going.

Each group's tasks are outlined on *Writing speech*. Hand these out to remind children.

Extra time

- Ask children to introduce a third person who has a differing viewpoint to the others.
- They can change direct speech to reported speech.
- Ask them to write an account of the match the two characters were going to.
- Ask children to repeat the question-and-answer process for when one of the characters arrives home and is asked about the match (i.e. recount through speech).

The analysis

Ask several children to **read their conversations out**.

Shoot-out

These targets might be highlighted and dated from this lesson's writing:

Secure 2 (2 children): 4.

High 2 (penguin on holiday): 4.

Low 3 (trainer): 1, 4.

Secure 3 (twirly flower): 1, 4, 10c.

High 3 (cup of tea): 3a, 3b, 3c.

Secure 4 (tiger saying "hello"): 1, 4b, 4c, 4d, 8.

4a (a bridge with a spider scurrying across it): 2.

FOOTBALL BUBBLE

Language-based learning favours girls. Lots of boys need kinaesthetic learning.

Writing speech

PPs

"Where are you going?" said Joe slowly.

Other words you could use . . .

screamed   yelled   answered

sadly   quickly   happily

Writing speech

CCs

"Where are you going?" Jatinder asked nosily.

Other words you could use . . .

sighed   screamed   yelled

curiously   annoyingly   irritatingly

Writing speech

DDs & LLs

"Where are you going?" Bob asked nosily.

- ■ Make your conversation tell a story.

- ■ Let the reader know what BOTH your characters think about the match (and make sure they disagree).

- ■ They are allowed to answer a question then ask one back straight away.

Organising research

level 2	Paperclip Premiers (PPs)
level 3c/3b	Chosen Champs (CCs)
level 3a/4c	Dream Division (DD)
level 4b/4a+	Longstop Leaguers (LLs)

Game plan

Children will: make notes from text and use them to write three paragraphs.

Training

For children

None.

For teachers

1 Eco-copy *In the beginning*, found on pages 24 and 25.
2 Eco-copy and chop *The history of Aston Villa Football Club* on pages 26 and 27, enough for footballers to share a copy.
3 Eco-copy and chop *The history of Cadbury's chocolate* on pages 28 and 29, enough for non-footballers to share a copy. Warning: photocopy extra Cadbury ones as team loyalty may well prevent some children choosing the football option.

The match

Warm-up

■ Give out the *History of Aston Villa and Cadbury* sheets. Ask children to work in pairs and **read the information** to each other – one being A, and the other being B.
■ Write "in the beginning," "key names" and "achievements" in different colours on the board. Ask children to take the same three colours (or make a key) and **underline relevant words in the text** in the correct colour.

First half

- Hand out *In the beginning*. Children should make "notes" in the boxes under each heading. However, they can only **write one word (or a whole date) in each box** – so children are limited in the number of words they can note.
- Discuss which words will not need to be written – *e.g. Aston Villa, chocolate, football, Cadbury's* – as children know these already.
- Explain that the word restriction is to stop children copying sentences, making them think instead about the most important words. This is an important life skill.

Half-time PEP talk

- Ask children to stand up. Call out a word (possibly in different voices) from the following list and ask children to **repeat the word**, then jump up and down three times before the next word is called out. These words and phrases are useful for explaining something in sequence:

  - *First of all*
  - *Next*
  - *After that*
  - *Then*
  - *Penultimate*
  - *Last*

  - *Introduction*
  - *Tell more*
  - *One side*
  - *The other side*
  - *Wrap it up.*

- Repeat if more practice is needed.

Second half

Collect in the *Aston Villa* or *Cadbury chocolate* information sheets. Ask children to **write three paragraphs** in their books, the opening phrase for each being written down beneath their note grids on *In the beginning*. They can use information they have remembered but should mainly use the words and notes they have in the grid.

Extra time

- Children can make notes in the same way on other non-fiction subjects.
- Children can research a topic to be used when writing a story.

The analysis

- Ask children to read out their sentences and **make a list of rules** to help them make notes in future. Include rules such as:

  - No sentences.
  - Use abbreviations.

- ▪ Read the information slowly.
- ▪ Make notes under headings.
- ▪ Key words only.
- ▪ No little words (like "and").

▪ Ask children to write out and complete this sentence:

I found this really (easy/hard) _____ because _____.

Shoot-out

Some targets are achieved with scaffolded support. For instance, low 3 (7) requires children to write a paragraph. Children should achieve that during this lesson. This is not the same as high 4 (3) which requires paragraphs to be used fluently throughout every piece of writing.

I CAN . . . targets children might have achieved today are:

High 2 (penguin on holiday): 7.

Low 3 (trainer): 7, 12.

Secure 3 (twirly flower): 6, 12.

High 3 (cup of tea): 9, 13.

Secure 4 (tiger saying "hello"): 6.

FOOTBALL BUBBLE

Many boys are desperate for peer approval.

In the beginning

In the beginning

Key names

Achievements

1   Aston Villa started when . . .

2   The important people were . . .

3   Aston Villa's greatest achievements are . . .

In the beginning

In the beginning

Key names

Achievements

1   Cadbury's started when . . .

2   The important people were . . .

3   Cadbury's greatest achievements are . . .

History of Aston Villa Football Club

PPs

(A) Aston Villa Football Club began when four friends watched a football match in February 1874.

(B) They formed a club. Players paid one shilling (5p) to Billy Mason to join.

(A) Fifteen people joined. Their very first match was against Aston Park Unity Team. Aston Villa won 1–0.

(B) They won the League Cup in 1994 and 1996.

History of Aston Villa Football Club

LLs

(A) Aston Villa Football Club began when Jack Hughes, Frederick Matthews, Walter Price and William Scattergood, who played cricket for a chapel team, watched a football match in February 1874.

(B) The four men thought that football could keep their chapel cricket team fit during winter. Those wishing to join the club paid one shilling (5p) to Billy Mason who became the first honorary secretary.

(A) Very soon, fifteen people had signed up and all played for the first team. One of the first matches was against Aston Park Unity Team. There were fourteen players on each side and play stopped when it became too dark to see the ball. Aston Villa won 1–0.

(B) The club won its first FA Cup in 1887.

(A) In 1888 the first football league was organised and Aston Villa was runner-up.

(B) It was 1920 before Aston Villa actually won the League.

(A) Aston Villa had to wait until 1957 before they won the FA Cup for the second time.

(B) Since then they have won the League Cup in 1994 and 1996.

History of Aston Villa Football Club

CCs

(A) Aston Villa Football Club began when Jack Hughes and three friends watched a football match in February 1874.

(B) They formed a club. Players paid one shilling (5p) to Billy Mason to join.

(A) Fifteen joined the club.

(B) One of the first games was against Aston Park Unity Team. Aston Villa won 1–0.

(A) It was 1920 before Aston Villa won the League.

(B) They won the League Cup in 1994 and 1996.

History of Aston Villa Football Club

DD

(A) Aston Villa Football Club started when Jack Hughes, William Scattergood and two friends from a chapel cricket team watched a football match in February 1874.

(B) The four men formed a club and players paid one shilling (5p) to Billy Mason to join.

(A) In the first year, fifteen people signed up and played for the first team.

(B) One of the first matches was against Aston Park Unity Team. There were fourteen players on each side. Aston Villa won 1–0.

(A) The club won its first FA Cup in 1887.

(B) It was 1920 before they actually won the League.

(A) It was 1957 before they won the FA Cup for the second time.

(B) Since then they have won the League Cup in 1994 and 1996.

History of Cadbury's chocolate

PPs

(A) In 1824 John Cadbury opened a shop in Birmingham. It became a chocolate factory.

(B) John Cadbury retired in 1861. His sons, Richard and George, took over from him.

(A) By 1878 Cadburys employed 200 workers so a bigger factory was found at Bournville, 4 miles south of the centre of Birmingham.

(B) Lastly, in 1895 Richard and George Cadbury bought land to build over 300 houses and schools for people who worked at the factory.

History of Cadbury's chocolate

LLs

(A) In 1824 John Cadbury opened a grocery shop in Bull Street, Birmingham.

(B) Within seven years the grocery shop had become a factory making drinking chocolate and cocoa and in 1847 it moved to a bigger building in Bridge Street.

(A) John Cadbury retired in 1861 and his sons Richard and George took over the business.

(B) By 1878, Cadburys employed 200 workers and a site for an even bigger factory was found at Bournville, 4 miles south of the centre of Birmingham. Land was also bought to build houses for the people who worked at the factory.

(A) George Gadd was the architect who worked on the new factory in September 1879. It was known as the "factory in a garden."

(B) By 1900 there were 313 cottages and plans for doctors, dentists, schools and swimming pools, and in 1906 the Cadburys introduced retirement pensions along with a Saturday half-day holiday and bank holidays.

History of Cadbury's chocolate

CCs

(A) In 1824 John Cadbury opened a grocery shop in Bull Street, Birmingham. It soon became a chocolate factory.

(B) When John Cadbury retired in 1861 his sons, Richard and George, took over running the factory.

(A) By 1878, Cadbury employed 200 workers and a site for an even bigger factory was found at Bournville, 4 miles south of the centre of Birmingham.

(B) Land was also bought to build houses for the people who worked at the factory.

(A) By 1900 there were 313 cottages and plans for doctors, dentists, schools and swimming pools.

(B) Six years later, in 1906, the Cadburys introduced a Saturday half-day holiday and bank holidays.

History of Cadbury's chocolate

DD

(A) In 1824 John Cadbury opened a grocery shop in Bull Street, Birmingham.

(B) Seven years later, in 1831, the grocery shop had become a factory where drinking chocolate and cocoa were made.

(A) By 1847 Cadburys had moved to a bigger building in Bridge Street.

(B) John Cadbury retired in 1861. His sons Richard and George took over from him.

(A) By 1878, Cadburys employed 200 workers and a site for an even bigger factory was found at Bournville, 4 miles south of the centre of Birmingham.

(B) Land was also bought to build houses for the people who worked at the factory.

(A) By 1900 there were 313 cottages and plans to build schools and swimming pools.

(B) Doctors and dentists were also part of the plans.

(A) In 1906, Cadburys began giving pensions to people who retired and also introduced a Saturday half-day holiday and bank holidays.

LESSON **6**

Verb diary

level 2	Paperclip Premiers (PPs)
level 3c/3b	Chosen Champs (CCs)
level 3a/4c	Dream Division (DD)
level 4b/4a+	Longstop Leaguers (LLs)

Game plan

Children will: use the correct verb tense in a short diary account.

Training

For children

None.

For teachers

1 Photocopy *Verbs tell you what people did/do/will do*, found on page 33, enough for one per child.
2 Find a picture of a place that a sports person, trainer, physiotherapist or journalist might go to, such as a stadium, swimming pool, cycle track, café, training ground, garage, shop.

The match

Warm-up

▪ In pairs, ask children to imagine they are sports players, trainers, physiotherapists or journalists. It is the day before a match and **they are preparing**. Act out what they do.
▪ Give PPs a picture suggesting a setting to help them focus and decide where their characters are. Also check that they know what a verb is.
▪ Give out *Verbs tell you what people did/do/will do* to each child.
▪ Ask children to **write verbs** for their characters in the past-tense column.

First half

■ In their books, ask children to **write phrases (not sentences) predicting what could possibly go wrong** on the day. Write this in the future tense in the right-hand (future) column:

> ■ *The car will break down.*
> ■ *The player will score an own goal.*
> ■ *The trainer will fall over in public.*
> ■ *A biased ref will spoil the game.*
> ■ *Snow will fall.*

■ Remind children that verbs in the future tenses are preceded by the words "will" or "is going to."

Half-time PEP talk

■ On the board, recreate the children's sheet with three columns headed "past," "present" and "future." **Write a list of verbs** – *throw, fling, swim, tear, catch, shoot, spend, leap, write* – in the middle/present-tense column, which apart from the first word is the same as children have on their own sheets.

■ Model what to do with the word "throw." Ask children to **stand up and move to their left**. This is past tense. So everyone says "threw." Children move one step to the right so are now back behind their chairs. This is present tense so say the word "throw." Now move one step to their right. This is future – "will throw." Children then pretend to throw something – *ball, javelin, frisbee.*

■ Repeat with the other words in the present column.

Second half

■ Ask children to add more present-tense verbs to the list in the central column.

■ Check these, then ask them to imagine they are their sports characters and **write a paragraph of a diary entry about the day** they were preparing for. This should be in the past tense.

■ When they have finished their paragraph, they should **underline every verb** in a coloured pencil and share entries with a friend.

Extra time

■ Children should rewrite their paragraphs in the present tense (only changing the verbs that have been underlined) and then the future tense.

■ They can write two newspaper articles about the same event; one written in anticipation of what will happen, the other in the past tense.

The analysis

At the bottom of each *I CAN . . .* sheet is an **"edit" section** to help children focus on something specific when editing their work. Ask children to read their own edit box, then take a different, coloured pencil and improve their writing by editing, looking for the suggestions in their edit boxes.

Shoot-out

Targets can be highlighted as follows:

Secure 2 (2 children): 3, 10.

Low 3 (trainer): 8.

Low 4 (man crawling out of a shark's mouth): 10a.

High 4 (bridge with spider crawling across it): 8.

FOOTBALL BUBBLE

By the age of three, girls are likely to have acquired nearly twice the vocabulary their male counterparts have.

Verbs tell you what people did/do/will do

Past (yesterday)	Present (today)	Future (tomorrow)
	fling	
	swim	
	tear (as in race)	
	catch	
	shoot	
	spend	
	leap	
	write	

The unexpected football match

level 2	Paperclip Premiers (PPs)
level 3c/3b	Chosen Champs (CCs)
level 3a/4c	Dream Division (DD)
level 4b/4a+	Longstop Leaguers (LLs)

Game plan

Children will: write a short poem about the 1914 trench football match with contrasting emotions, powerful verbs, adverbs and onomatopoeias – suitable for 11 November, UK Armistice Day.

Training

For children

None.

For teachers

1 Photocopy *The unexpected football match* on page 37, one between two.
2 Eco-copy the *War poem* scaffolds on pages 38 and 39.
3 Find a German dictionary (optional).
4 Locate pictures of the First World War trenches.

The match

Warm-up

- Ask children to think of **onomatopoeias for sounds they might hear at a football match** and write them down on their whiteboards.
- Divide the board into three columns and record some of the best onomatopoeias in the middle column. Note that a row of adverbs are later going to be added along the bottom of the board, so leave enough room for a row of words underneath.
- Show children pictures of soldiers in trenches and explain what **No Man's Land** was (it is important later on in the lesson).
- Ask them to make up onomatopoeic sounds soldiers might have heard. A lot of these will need exclamation marks. Recap when these need to be used.

- Record these words in the column on the left.
- In the right-hand column write words that represent **stillness**. Make sure some words with phonic sounds (*sh*, *s*, soft *c* and *th*) in them – *hush*, *peace*, *nothingness* – are in the list.

First half

- Hand out *Unexpected football match* and together **read the true account** of what happened in the trenches in 1914.
- Explore how the children feel about what happened.
- Ask a child to come to the front and be a soldier (German or English). Hot-seat the child to find out what it was like to play in the match, how feelings and opinions changed and what conditions were like.

Half-time PEP talk

- Recap the definition of an **adverb**, then ask six children to make a line at the front of the classroom. Working along the line, ask each child to demonstrate how to "perform" a **different verb** that might describe what happened in the trenches or at a football match in an adverb style – *e.g. run (on the spot) slowly, jump quickly, wave enthusiastically, bellow loudly*.
- Work along the row once more with everyone now standing up and joining in.

Second half

- Write the adverbs used in HALF-TIME PEP TALK along the bottom of the board. Add some further ones if time allows.
- Now ask children to **write a poem** (not necessarily in verses) in four parts about the 1914 football match. The *War Poem* scaffold will help children with their writing.
- Encourage LLs and DDs to include rhetorical questions.
- Non-football writers can focus on the exchange of presents.

Extra time

- Copy edited poems out and illustrate to make a class anthology or for display purposes. Laminating published poems will help the book last longer and makes it more "special."

- Rewrite poems in prose.

- Read Michael Foreman's *War Game* (published by Puffin) or watch the film of the book as it is based on the 1914 Christmas football match.

- Research further information about the First World War. Develop poetry ideas using technical vocabulary.

The analysis

Ask children to **share their poems** with a partner or the class.

Shoot-out

The following *I CAN* . . . statements might have been achieved . . .

> Low 2 (funny face): 7.
>
> Secure 2 (2 children): 4, 6a.
>
> High 2 (penguin on holiday): 1, 4, 5a.
>
> Low 3 (trainer): 1, 4, 8.
>
> Secure 3 (twirly flower): 1, 3, 4, 5.
>
> High 3 (cup of tea): 3a, 3b, 3c, 3d, 4, 5.
>
> Low 4 (man crawling out of a shark's mouth): 10a.
>
> Secure 4 (tiger saying "hello"): 4a, 4b, 4c, 4d, 8, 12, 15.
>
> High 4 (bridge with spider scurrying across it): 1, 2.
>
> Level 5 (Nigel the gnome about to eat his breakfast): 11.

FOOTBALL BUBBLE

Visual learners do better if words they need to manipulate are written down.

An unexpected football match

It was cold, so numbingly cold; and muddy, and horrible, and nearly Christmas. German soldiers shivered as winter's ice-cold fingernails dug into their muscles. The trench was 2 metres deep. Shards of frozen snow lay at the bottom of it. That was where they were meant to sleep.

One hundred metres away, guns loaded and pointing at the Germans, English soldiers shuddered as a chill wind wound its way round *their* trench. They, too, lived with ice and rats and filth and . . . The lookout at the top of the English trench blinked twice, then squinted his eyes to make sure he really had seen what he thought he had seen.

Those Germans had lifted a Christmas tree with a lighted candle out of their trench. It flickered in the darkness. Now there was another tree and more candles and before long the trench top was a twinkling forest. The lookout called for his mates. They joined him, mesmerised by the lights and . . . the singing. German words, but the tune was the same; a Christmas carol they knew – "Silent night, holy night" a song about God sending his son to live on earth to bring peace. In this place where men were ordered to shoot each other?

Yet it happened. Some German soldiers had worked in England before the war. Before long a board was hoisted above the German trench. "YOU NO FIGHT, WE NO FIGHT" it read. That was just the beginning.

As daylight came, troops climbed out of their trenches and crossed the land between them. No Man's Land became Friends' Land. They shook hands, exchanged chocolate cake, newspapers, postcards. And then someone produced a football. Someone would, wouldn't they?

And so began a bizarre game – England versus Germany, playing in the freezing cold, surrounded by barbed wire and holes where shells had exploded. There was no referee, no game plan, just two groups of soldiers who thought there were better things to do than fire guns at each other. Today they would shoot goals. Eventually they returned back to their trenches.

It should not have happened. The British major in charge of the trench troops said it most definitely should not have happened. The German commanders felt the same. Both removed the football players, replaced them with hardened, tough soldiers who were hungry for blood.

So once more, cold metal bullets ripped into human flesh.

War poem

PPs

Part 1 – *Soldiers hate each other*:

They are busy, angry, loud. Make your lines short. Use powerful verbs and harsh letter sounds (like *k*, hard *g*, *b*). Use words that need exclamation marks.

Part 2 – *Soldiers meet each other*:

Use soft-sounding words, longer phrases and lines. Put in commas and full stops to slow the poem down. Describe the football match and sharing presents.

Part 3 – *Soldiers refuse to shoot at each other*:

All is still. Imagine you are whispering the words as you write them. Describe the weather.

Part 4 – *Officers bark*:

Write in short lines (like at the beginning of the poem). The officers are telling the troops to fire at each other. This makes a huge contrast with the silence and stillness in the previous lines.

     © Heather Butler 2010 *Literacy in Action: Football* Routledge

War poem

CCs, DD, LLs

Part 1 – *Soldiers hate each other*:

They are busy, angry, loud. Make your lines short. Use powerful verbs and harsh letter sounds (like *k*, hard *g*, *b*). Use words that need exclamation marks and technical words to do with war. Think about using a metaphor or simile.

Part 2 – *Soldiers meet each other*:

Use speech (don't forget the speech marks), soft-sounding words, longer phrases and lines. Use German words if you know any. Put in commas and full stops to slow the poem down. Describe the football match and sharing presents.

Part 3 – *Soldiers refuse to shoot at each other*:

All is still. Imagine you are whispering the words as you write them. Describe the weather. Use a rhetorical question to draw the reader in.

Part 4 – *Officers bark*:

Write in short lines (like at the beginning of the poem) telling the troops to fire. This makes a huge contrast with the silence and stillness in the previous lines. End your poem with a question.

Programmed for success

level 2	Paperclip Premiers (PPs)
level 3c/3b	Chosen Champs (CCs)
level 3a/4c	Dream Division (DD)
level 4b/4a+	Longstop Leaguers (LLs)

Game plan

Children will: use connectives and write an article for a programme with the reader in mind.

Training

For children

Bring in programmes of sports or other (e.g. theatre) events.

For teachers

1 Find some programmes.
2 Eco-copy the *Programme* sheet on pages 43 and 44, enough for one per child.

The match

Warm-up

Look at the programmes children have brought in and allow space to talk about them. Programmes are written by people who earn money from writing – learning to write is a good thing to do!

First half

- Give children a timed 2 minutes to make a list on their whiteboards of **different genres** of writing in the programme – *letters, lists, reviews, jokes, biographies, calendars, advertising forthcoming events, children's pages.*
- Now make a **communal list of genres** on the left-hand side of the board. For each genre suggested, ask the child who suggested it to stand up. When about ten children are standing, recap answers by naming a child and seeing if others can remember their genre. If it is remembered correctly, the child standing up sits down.

Half-time PEP talk

- On the right-hand side of the board, ask children to contribute to a **list of connectives**. DDs and LLs should also be able to think of **connective phrases** – *"in the meantime," "while he was out."*
- Now children should stand up and **work down the connective words** one at a time, running on the spot for 5 seconds between each word. This works best if the running is very vigorous for 5 seconds, everyone stops and stands tall until the teacher points to the next word (not necessarily in sequential order) and specifies how it is to be said – e.g. *"like a grumpy old crocodile with a sore head," "like an angry giant."* Invite children to say how the connective is to be said as well. As connectives are often short words, they may need to be repeated to create an impact and to give the children a chance to enjoy the mini-roleplay moment.

Second half

Hand out the *Programme* sheet. In their books, ask children to **write for the programme**. They can choose any genre they like, including genres not on the board. They have been told who their audience is and also what they need to include.

Extra time

- Ask children to write a further article for a programme.

- They should go through a programme and make a detailed list of the types of genre found there. Then children should order the list, with the genre they think would be easiest to write at the top. State their reasons for top and bottom choices. Now write both and see if they still think that.

- Ask children to make a programme for a forthcoming school event.

The analysis

- Ask children to **share their writing** with a partner.
- This lesson would be a really good opportunity to highlight some *I CAN . . .* targets.

41

Shoot-out

Targets that might have been achieved during the writing task are:

Low 2 (funny face): 2, 8.

Secure 2 (2 children): 1, 2.

High 2 (penguin on holiday): 2, 3, 8, 11.

Low 3 (trainer): 2, 3.

Secure 3 (twirly flower): 2.

High 3 (a cup of tea): 2, 3b, 5, 11.

Low 4 (man crawling out of a shark's mouth): 1, 9.

Secure 4 (tiger saying "hello"): 2, 8, 14.

Level 5 (Nigel the gnome about to eat his breakfast): 3, 4, 5, 6.

FOOTBALL BUBBLE

Boys need to know why they are learning to do things and how it will help them in the future. This is particularly important if the task is a difficult one.

Programme

PPs

My audience is . . .
> a child aged 6

So I will . . .

- ◼ Write short sentences that have capital letters and full stops.

- ◼ Make the beginning of every sentence different.

- ◼ Use the words **and**, **but**, and **then** to make two sentences longer.

Programme

CCs

My audience is . . .
> a mum aged 32

So I will . . .

- ◼ Make the beginning of every sentence different (mums like that).

- ◼ Use the words **because**, **as**, **then**, **so**, and **although** to make my sentences longer.

- ◼ Write about something a mum would be interested in – such as planning a trip with her children.

Programme

DD

My audience is . . .

a 13-year-old who loves long sentences

So I will . . .

- ■ Use these connectives – **and**, **but**, **as**, **then**, **so**, **because**, **although**, **however**.

- ■ Include a list with commas between each word, and the word "and" before the last word – e.g. Hull, Leeds, Sheffield and Barnsley.

- ■ Give an opinion about something.

Programme

LLs

My audience is . . .

a retired man or woman (with grandchildren)

So I will . . .

- ■ Include a description of something using several different connectives such as **although**, **however**, **if**, and **because**.

- ■ Include a connective phrase at the beginning of at least one sentence such as **there again**, **in the meantime**.

- ■ Give an opinion about something.

Walter Tull

level 2	Paperclip Premiers (PPs)
level 3c/3b	Chosen Champs (CCs)
level 3a/4c	Dream Division (DD)
level 4b/4a+	Longstop Leaguers (LLs)

Game plan

Children will: use ideas taken from text to produce an account of a character's life using writing that has a distinct opening and ending – suitable for work promoting black/ethnic personalities.

Training

For children

None.

For teachers

1 Eco-copy the *Key sheet*, as found on pages 48–50, to be shared one between two.
2 Photocopy appropriate sheets about *Walter Tull's life* for each child, as found on pages 51–54.

The match

Warm-up

▦ Give out the *Key sheet* and ask children for **examples of each of the categories**.
▦ Ask children to **create and write a symbol** in the column next to the category on their sheet. For example . . .

  ▦ *Job (e.g. briefcase)*
  ▦ *Place (e.g. little house or building with distinctive shape)*
  ▦ *Year (e.g. clock)*
  ▦ *Sentence (e.g. capital letter and full stop)*
  ▦ *Adverb (e.g. shooting star)*
  ▦ *Connective (e.g. two rectangular magnets)*

■ *Words in brackets to clarify something (e.g. brackets outside a smiley face)*
■ *Words written to show how the writer feels about something (e.g. thought bubble)*

First half

■ **Read out the PP version of *Walter Tull's life*.**
■ **Recap key facts**, then give out the appropriate sheets about *Walter Tull's life*. Ask children to read it in pairs, and in the left-hand column they should **use their symbols** from the *Key sheets* to show where the categories can be found.

Half-time PEP talk

■ Ask children to suggest **different stages of life** from birth to death. Stand behind chairs and create a physical symbol for each stage.
■ If writing about someone's life, there is an obvious beginning, ending and sequenced structure. Explain how this can be made better by introducing **something in the beginning that is referred to at the end**; this "glues" the beginning and end of the piece together. Objects, weather, colours and dates are all good "glues."

> ■ *A baby boy is given a teddy bear. When he dies, his family find the bear in a box.*
> ■ *The sun is shining when someone is born and also shines over his or her gravestone as another character reads it.*
> ■ *A baby girl is wrapped in a yellow blanket, the same colour as the blanket on her bed when she dies.*
> ■ *Someone is born and dies on a Tuesday.*

■ In pairs, see if children (and especially DDs and LLs) can think of "glues."

Second half

■ Ask children to **create a character** (such as a sports personality, pet, family member, book character) and write about his or her life in a similar style to the text about Walter Tull – beginning (birth), information about where he or she lived, childhood, significant events in his or her life, ending (death).
■ Use the right-hand column on the *Key sheet* to **jot down details and words or phrases** that will be used in the writing task before beginning to write.

Extra time

Invite children to write a further character description told from a biased viewpoint.

The analysis

Ask children to read through their writing and **underline and write symbols** from *Key sheets* in the appropriate place in their writing.

Shoot-out

These *I CAN* . . . targets may have been met:

Low 2 (funny face): 2.

Secure 2 (2 children): 1, 5.

High 2 (penguin on holiday): 3, 9.

Low 3 (trainer): 7, 13.

Secure 3 (twirly flower): 1, 6, 13.

High 3 (cup of tea): 2, 3, 6, 7.

Low 4 (man crawling out of a shark's mouth): 3, 8, 9, 11.

Secure 4 (tiger saying "hello"): 3, 7, 9, 14, 15.

High 4 (a bridge with a spider scurrying across it): 2, 3, 10, 11.

Low 5 (Nigel the gnome about to eat his breakfast): 4, 10, 12, 13.

FOOTBALL BUBBLE

Female sex hormones lower aggression, competition, self-assertion and self-reliance . . .

Key sheet

PPs

Year		
Job		
Place		
New sentence		1 Born 2 Important things that happened 3 Died

Key sheet

CCs

Family		
Year		
Job		
Place		
Adverb		
New paragraph		1 Born (beginning) 2 Important things that happened 3 Died (ending)

Key sheet

DD

Family		
Year		
Job		
Place		
Adverb		
Connective		
New paragraph		1 Born (beginning) 2 Childhood 3 Important things that happened when he or she was an adult 4 Died (ending)

Key sheet

LLs

Family		
Job		
Place		
Adverb		
Connective words in brackets to make something clearer		
Show what you think about his or her life all the way through your writing		

Walter Tull's life

PPs

Walter Tull was one of the first black footballers to earn money playing football in Britain.

Walter was born in April 1888. Sadly, his mother and father died when he was a child. Walter was sent to an orphanage in London.

In 1908, Walter started playing for Clapton. That year they won three cups.

Spurs then bought him for £10 and he was paid £4 a week.

In 1910 he played for Northampton Town. He played over 100 games for them.

The First World War broke out in 1914. Walter Tull joined the British army.

He died in France on 25 March 1918, hit by a bullet.

Walter Tull's life

CCs

Walter Tull was one of the first black football players in Britain.

He was born in April 1888. Sadly, his mother died when he was seven and his father two years later. Walter was sent to an orphanage in London.

By the beginning of the 1908–9 season, Walter was playing for the first football team at Clapton. That year they won three cups.

Tottenham Hotspur bought him for £10 and he was paid £4 a week. He played in the first division (same as the premier division now), mostly in the reserves team.

The following year he moved to Northampton Town where he played over 100 games and became the club's most popular player.

When the First World War broke out in 1914, Walter Tull joined the army. He became an officer in 1917, the first black officer ever in the British army.

He died on 25 March 1918, hit by a bullet as he led his men out of the trenches towards enemy lines.

Walter Tull's life

DD

Walter Tull was the second black football player to earn money playing football in Britain. The first was Arthur Wharton who played for Preston North End.

Walter Tull's grandfather had been a slave and his father came to England in 1876. Walter was born in Kent in April 1888. Sadly, his mother died when he was seven and his father two years later, so Walter and his brother Edward were sent to a Christian orphanage in London.

By the beginning of the 1908–9 season, Walter was playing for the first football team at Clapton. That year they won three cups. One newspaper said, "He was the catch of the season".

Tottenham Hotspur bought him for £10 and he was paid £4 a week. He played in the first division (the same as the premier division now). His team lost their first match against Sunderland, 3–1, then the second against Everton, but drew the third 2–2 against Manchester United.

That season, Walter Tull played mostly in the reserves team and the following year he transferred to Northampton Town where he played over a hundred games and became the club's most popular player.

When the First World War broke out in 1914, Walter Tull joined the army. Because he was a good leader, he was promoted to become an officer in 1917, the first black officer ever in the British army.

He died fighting in France on 25 March 1918, hit by a bullet as he bravely led his men out of the trenches towards enemy lines.

Walter Tull's life

LLs

Walter Tull was the second black football player to play professionally in Britain. The first was Arthur Wharton who played for Preston North End in 1886.

Walter Tull's grandfather had been a slave in Barbados and his father came to England in 1876. Walter was born in Folkestone (in Kent) in April 1888. Sadly, his mother died when he was seven and his father two years later. Walter and his brother Edward were sent to a Christian orphanage in Bethnal Green, London.

When he left school Walter worked as a printer, but by the beginning of the 1908–9 season he was playing for the first football team at Clapton. Thanks to him (he was their top goal scorer) they won the Amateur Cup, the London Senior Cup and the London County Amateur Cup. The *Football Star* newspaper said he was the "catch of the season".

From Clapton he moved to Tottenham Hotspur for a £10 signing fee. He was paid £4 a week and played in the first division (now called the Premier Division). He lost his first match against Sunderland, 3–1, and his second against Everton, but drew the third 2–2 against Manchester United.

A writer in the *Daily Chronicle* rightly described him as playing with perfect coolness, carefully waiting for a fraction of a second in order to get a pass in with accuracy. Despite such wonderful descriptions he was mostly in the reserves team and only played seven times in the first team that season. The following year he transferred to Northampton Town where he played over a hundred games and became the club's most popular player.

When the First World War broke out in 1914, Walter Tull joined the army and was promoted to sergeant in 1916. He became an officer in 1917, the first black officer ever in the British army. He died on 25 March 1918, hit by a bullet as he bravely led his men out of the trenches towards enemy lines. He was a real hero and achieved amazing things during his short life.

Fiddle's injury

level 2	Paperclip Premiers (PPs)
level 3c/3b	Chosen Champs (CCs)
level 3a/4c	Dream Division (DD)
level 4b/4a+	Longstop Leaguers (LLs)

Game plan

Children will: find small words inside longer ones, list technical words related to injuries and write a biased newspaper article which includes technical words.

Training

For children

None.

For teachers

1 Eco-copy *Fiddle's injury* on page 58 and cut it up ready for use, one per child.
2 Locate enough thesauruses for everyone.

The match

Warm-up

▪ Give out *Fiddle's injury* sheets. Talk through the example of "capital" then ask children to find **as many "three letters or more" words in each of the longer words** in the top right-hand box. Letters must be sequential. The number of words to look for is shown in brackets.

  ▪ *PPs: minimum (1) – mum; carrot (2) – car, rot.*
  ▪ *CCs: fearless (3) – fear, less, ear; something (4) – some, thing, met, thin.*
  ▪ *DDs: equipment (3) – equip, quip, men; interesting (5) – interest, rest, tin, sting, ting.*
  ▪ *LLs: favourite (3) – favour, our, rite; photograph (5) – photo, graph, tog, rap, hot; lampstand (5) – lamp, stand, amp, amps, and (Stan is not allowed as it is a name and needs a capital letter).*

First half

Introduce Fern/Fernando Fiddle, who is an injured sports player. In pairs, ask children to decide which injury Fiddle has.

The injury means that movement is now awkward. Ask children to decide which part of their character's body is injured and how. If children know "technical" words (e.g. *hamstring, femur, cartilage*), then use these.

Half-time PEP talk

Ask children to **walk round the classroom** as their injured character would.

Second half

- Quieten any hilarity and ask children to **write down three verbs** on their whiteboards to describe how they moved, in a list. Now **use thesauruses to add another three** words.
- Share the children's favourite verbs and **make a word bank** on the board.
- Ask children to decide whether they are **sympathetic or cynical** about Fiddle's injury, and discuss why with a partner.
- Read out the following three sentences and ask children to say how the biased point of view is shown.

  - *Fiddle hobbled bravely despite having torn most of the ligaments in his right ankle.*
  - *Fiddle's netball days were numbered following her horrific injury when she collided with the opposition's goal defence.*
  - *Fiddle lumbered like an egocentric turtle towards the referee after the fall; he wasn't injured, so what was he making such a fuss about?*

- Children should **write an article for a newspaper** about the injury from a biased viewpoint, letting the reader know what they think about the injured sportsperson. Expect LLs to give examples of what their character has done to back up their favour or dislike.

Extra time

- Using the edit suggestions on their *I CAN* . . . target sheets, children should read through their article and improve it.

- They should rewrite the article from a different viewpoint.

The analysis

Ask children to reread their writing and, using a coloured pencil, **underline longer words with smaller words inside** – as in the WARM-UP. The number of words children should look for is in the bottom left box of *Fiddle's injury*.

Shoot-out

Check off targets as follows:

Low 2 (funny face): 5.

Secure 2 (2 children): 10.

High 2 (penguin on holiday): 7, 10.

Low 3 (trainer): 10.

Secure 3 (twirly flower): 11.

Low 4 (man crawling out of a shark's mouth): 4.

Secure 4 (tiger saying "hello"): 12, 16.

Level 5 (Nigel the gnome about to eat his breakfast): 13.

FOOTBALL BUBBLE

Using technical words helps convince the reader that writers know their subject.

Fiddle's injury

PPs

Warm-up	capital (2) = cap + pit minimum (1) carrot (2)
3	

CCs

Warm-up	capital (2) = cap + pit fearless (3) something (4)
5	

DD

Warm-up	capital (2) = cap + pit equipment (3) interesting (5)
7	

LLs

Warm-up	capital (2) = cap + pit favourite (3) photograph (5) lampstand (5)
10	

Speaking of pronouns

level 2	Paperclip Premiers (PPs)
level 3c/3b	Chosen Champs (CCs)
level 3a/4c	Dream Division (DD)
level 4b/4a+	Longstop Leaguers (LLs)

Game plan

Children will: correctly match verbs and pronouns, use speech punctuation and think of different ways to describe speech, including adverbs.

Training

For children

None.

For teachers

1 Photocopy and enlarge one copy of the *Pronoun list* on page 62. Chop it up into individual slips.
2 Eco-copy the *Speech marks* sheet on page 63 and cut it up, one each for PP, one between two for everyone else.
3 Write the witty ditty in HALF-TIME PEP TALK on the board before the lesson begins.

The match

Warm-up

▦ Remind children **what pronouns are** and how they abbreviate nouns. Pronouns also have to match the verb they are paired with.
▦ **Play pop-up pronouns**. Give each child a pronoun from the *Pronoun list*. Let DDs and LLs work with the less well-known ones in the latter part of the list.
▦ Read out the sentences below. When children's pronouns could go in the silent gap they "pop up" out of their seats and, when asked, call out their pronoun. For most of the sentences, several children should pop up at the same time.

- The sportsperson hung up ___ boots.
- Look after ___.
- They enjoyed ___.
- ___ went to the match.

- "That's ___ ," said the referee.
- The manager picked ___ up.
- ___ are going to the match.
- __ took ___ to the café.

First half

- On the board, draw a coach (person, not vehicle) and a speech bubble saying words he or she might use to instruct his or her players. E.g., *"You are going to do forty press-ups . . ."*; *"Take yourselves round the pitch five times . . ."*
- On their whiteboards, ask children to **draw a speech bubble and write further instructions** that must use the pronoun they were given in the WARM-UP.
- Children should check that speech sentences are good ones by reading them with a partner.
- Do not clean whiteboards.

Half-time PEP talk

Say the following witty ditty while **running on the spot**:

Pronouns stick to verbs like glue; ours, his, theirs, mine, you
He jumps, she sings, we wave, they chew; pronouns stick to verbs like glue.

Second half

- Particularly for PPs, recap how to add **speech punctuation** correctly. If you want to do this with actions, refer to lesson 4 for suggested actions for each part of the punctuation process.
- Ask children to write the words inside the **speech bubbles currently on their whiteboards in their books** with speech marks round them. **Add verbs**, and then adverbs as well to show how the words are spoken: *he growled*; *she whispers sneakily*.
- **Peer check** that punctuation has been correctly used and interesting ways of speaking have been indicated.
- Ask children to **write a series of spoken statements** the coach might make. Each group must include the examples given on *Speech marks*.

Extra time

- Ask children to write a paragraph about what the coach was doing using only pronouns and no names, then read it out and see how confusing it is. They should rewrite with nouns.

- Ask children to turn the direct speech into reported speech.

- They should place all cut-out pronouns from WARM-UP face down on a table, then pick one up and invent a sentence that includes the pronoun.

The analysis

▪ Recap how pronouns have to match with the verb. Using a different-coloured pencil for each pronoun/verb set, **draw circles round pronouns and partner verbs** and join them together with a single line.

▪ OR – say the following sentences and see if children can correctly punctuate them on their whiteboards:

  ▪ *Kenny screamed, "pick up that stick."*
  ▪ *"Throw me the ball," Aaran shouted.*
  ▪ *"Tomorrow," Tania yelled, "I'm going to make you run ten times round the pitch."*

Shoot-out

High 2 (penguin on holiday): 4

Low 3 (trainer): 1

Secure 3 (twirly flower): 1, 4

High 3 (cup of tea): 3a, 3b

Low 4 (man crawling out of a shark's mouth): 10b

Secure 4 (tiger saying "hello"): 4b, 4c, 8

High 4 (bridge with a spider scurrying across it): 2, 7

FOOTBALL BUBBLE

A female resting brain maintains around 90% of its electrical activity. Resting male brains maintain about 30% and shut down 70% . . .

Pronoun list

he	she	they
you	me	her
him	it	us
them	I	we
yours	their	hers
his	ours	this
that	these	those
who	theirs	what
myself	yourself	mine
anyone	nobody	some
everything	everyone	many
somebody	anybody	themselves

© Heather Butler 2010 *Literacy in Action: Football* Routledge

Speech marks

PPs

Practise putting speech marks correctly on the sheet then copy the sentences out in your books. Don't forget the full stops.
Now add an adverb to each sentence.

- Hold my hand he shouted
- Your boots are old she said
- Do not move it they yelled
- Give those to us everyone whispered

Speech marks

CCs, DD

In each sentence show off how to use:

- a pronoun
- an interesting verb for "said"
- an adverb to describe how words were said.

Speech marks

LLs

In each sentence show off how to use:

- A pronoun.
- An interesting verb for "said".
- An adverb to describe how words were said.
- Some form of punctuation to show expression, such as italics, capital letters, exclamation and question marks. *E.g.*, "YOU will do twenty-five *sit*-ups!" barked Franko.

Storytime – planning

level 2	Paperclip Premiers (PPs)
level 3c/3b	Chosen Champs (CCs)
level 3a/4c	Dream Division (DD)
level 4b/4a+	Longstop Leaguers (LLs)

Lessons 12, 13 and 14, taught together, give children time to plan, research, write, edit and publish a five-part, structured story. These three lessons will easily spread to a whole week's work.

Game plan

Children will: research and plan a paragraphed story using a simple scaffold.

Training

For children

Ask them to bring in non-fiction books or other means of research (e.g. printed pages from the Internet) about something they would like to write a story about.

For teachers

1 Enlarge to A3, photocopy, possibly laminate, and cut up the words inside the *Chair words* grids on pages 68–69.
2 Do the same with the *Quick story ideas* grids on pages 70–71.
3 Photocopy the *Scaffold* on page 72 for PPs and CCs.
4 Find some non-fiction books for those who forget.
5 Put five chairs in a row at the front of the classroom.
6 Music and mode of playing it if doing musical chairs in HALF-TIME PEP TALK.

The match

Warm-up

▪ Suggest to children that when they were younger they wrote what they thought were stories, such as:

> 1 *I went to the park.*
> 2 *I fell over.*
> 5 *I went home.*

▪ Using the chopped-up words from *Chair words (park)*, **give children the correct strips** and ask them to sit down on the first, second and fifth chairs at the front of the classroom, holding the strips so that everyone else can see them.

▪ But they were not writing stories – they were writing recounts. A story must have a dilemma/crisis/problem/climax/challenge (whichever word children are familiar with), that is then solved.

▪ Ask two more children to come to the front and sit on the third and fourth chairs, holding the last two *Chair words (park)*.

> 1 *I went to the park.*
> 2 *A dog was there.*
> 3 *The dog jumped at me.*
> 4 *A man chased it away.*
> 5 *I went home.*

First half

▪ **Replace the cut-up *Chair words (park)*** with the cut up *Chair words (story structure)* showing the five stages of a story.

> 1 *Someone does something.*
> 2 *Add more detail.*
> 3 *Something goes wrong.*
> 4 *It's sorted out.*
> 5 *Move on.*

▪ **Hand out one of the chopped-up *Quick story ideas*** to five children. Ask them to work out which part of the story they have been given and stand in the correct place behind the children sitting on the chairs holding up the five story stages.

▪ Ask someone to read out the story and check that it makes sense.

▪ **Swap the standing-up children** with those on the chairs (who return to their normal seats), collect in the *Quick story ideas* and repeat with other *Quick story ideas*. What to include in part 3, the dilemma, can be remembered by the mnemonic LID – there must be a Loss, an Injury or a Disappointment.

Half-time PEP talk

Repeat the five parts of *Chair words (story structure)* while jogging on the spot OR play musical chairs where children move to music until the music stops, when they must sit down on the floor and repeat the five story parts. The children that sit down should repeat part 1 (someone does something) several times, the second should "add more detail," and so on.

Second half

- In their books children are going to use the five part-plan to **create their own story plan**. To help them think of ideas and use good vocabulary, they are going to use non-fiction books. Expect CCs, DDs and LLs to **record their research with headings** for easy reference. Put these headings on the board to help: "*great technical words*," "*facts*," "*ideas I can recycle*."
- For the last heading, encourage children to think of an idea they have read in a fiction book. Real writers do this all the time. The easiest one is directly to lift a character from a fiction book and give him or her a new name.
- Children should **plan what will happen in their stories using the** *scaffold*.

Extra time

- Ask children to think of similes, metaphors and rhetorical questions that could be included.

- Children should work in pairs and tell one another what is going to happen in their story.

- Encourage them to complete further research.

The analysis

Ask children to **write a sentence about how useful the five-part plan** was and why.

Shoot-out

High 2 (penguin on holiday): 7.

Low 3 (trainer): 6, 12.

Secure 3 (twirly flower): 9, 12.

High 3 (cup of tea): 9, 13.

Low 4 (man crawling out of a shark's mouth): 4, 5.

Secure 4 (tiger saying "hello"): 6, 7, 12.

High 4 (bridge with a spider scurrying across it): 4.

Level 5 (Nigel the gnome about to eat his breakfast): 9.

FOOTBALL BUBBLE

Boys will focus on "fight or flight" more readily than girls if threatened. A gentle approach will often keep boys on task more effectively than confrontation.

Chair words (park)

1 I went to the park.

2 A dog was there.

3 The dog jumped at me.

4 A man chased it away.

5 I went home.

Chair words (story structure)

1 Someone does something.

2 Add more detail.

3 Something goes wrong.

4 It's sorted out.

5 Move on.

Quick story ideas (swimming – loss)

There is a swimming gala.
The home team expects to win.
Someone's swimming costume/trunks are ripped/stolen/lost.
Mike Spark the swimming pool manager finds a spare pair.
The swimming gala carries on and the home team come second.

Quick story ideas (football – injury)

The football team is playing.
They are about to win the league.
Their top scorer is injured.
The sub scores instead.
Half of the stadium is happy.

Scaffold

Five paragraphs **Plan what happens:**	**Plan the words you will use**: technical words, great adjectives, strong verbs
1 **Someone does something.**	
2 **Add more detail.**	
3 **Something goes wrong.**	
4 **It's sorted out – think of up to three things that might stop it being sorted out.**	
5 **Move on.**	

Storytime – writing

level 2	Paperclip Premiers (PPs)
level 3c/3b	Chosen Champs (CCs)
level 3a/4c	Dream Division (DD)
level 4b/4a+	Longstop Leaguers (LLs)

This lesson should be taught in conjunction with lessons 12 and 14.

Game plan

Children will: write a story in structured paragraphs using notes from research.

Training

For children

None.

For teachers

1 Think about whether to provide keyboards for some children to write.
2 Quiet music (without words) and means to play it.

The match

Warm-up

Check *I CAN . . .* targets that still need achieving as this is an ideal opportunity for children to "show off" their writing skills. Ask children to **choose two** they will try to achieve in the process of writing, editing and publishing their story. Encourage them to choose one target that is skill-based and one to do with presentation.

First half

- Without picking up a pencil, children should **reread research and planning notes** done in lesson 12.
- Children should share with a partner what is going to happen in each of the five stages of their story. Each of these stages will be a paragraph.
- Remind children about writing **interesting opening sentences and paragraphs** to draw the reader in, and ask children to share some of the **strong verbs and powerful adjectives** they have written down in their scaffold plans.
- Decide whether some children may achieve more if they use a **keyboard** to write.
- Ask all children to **write on alternate lines** as this will make editing much easier. They should also write in **pencil**.
- Lastly, ask them to think of **who their story is for** (e.g. my mum, my little brother, a story in a programme for a football match) and write this at the top of their page.
- A title will be chosen after the story has been written.
- Quiet music is often useful to help children focus.
- **Begin writing.**

Half-time PEP talk

- When children become restless, stop everyone writing and ask them to **read their story to a partner** (for approval) and to rehearse orally what is going to happen next.
- Ask them to stand up behind their chairs, **jump up and down ten times**, then give the biggest cheer ever.

Second half

Remind children of their own *I CAN* . . . targets and check to see if they have achieved them yet. **Continue writing.**

Extra time

- Children should read through stories to find words that could be improved.

- Real writers often leave their writing for several days, weeks, months or even years before returning to it. Children can't do this unless their work is filed away and brought back out months later. If this is an option, save completed stories (published in lesson 14) for when their stories are resurrected.

The analysis

- Children should **read their favourite two sentences** to a partner and say why they are favourites.
- Ask children if they have written something they are proud of – or something they have never felt confident writing before. Read these out to the class.
- Children should think of **a title** for their stories.

Shoot-out

In this instance a complete list of writing-skill *I CAN* . . . targets that may have been achieved is given, for a feast of achievement:

Low 2 (funny face): 2, 3, 4, 7, 8.

Secure 2 (2 children): 1, 2, 3, 4, 5, 6, 13.

High 2 (penguin on holiday): 1, 2, 3, 4, 5a, 5b, 7, 8, 9, 11.

Low 3 (trainer): 1, 2, 3, 4, 6, 7, 8, 9, 13.

Secure 3 (twirly flower): 1, 2, 3, 4, 5, 6, 9, 10, 11, 13.

High 3 (cup of tea): 1, 2, 3, 4, 5, 6, 7, 9, 11, 12.

Low 4 (man crawling out of a shark's mouth): 1, 2, 3, 4, 5, 8, 9, 10, 11.

Secure 4 (tiger saying "hello"): 1, 3, 4, 6, 7, 8, 9, 10, 12, 13, 14, 15.

High 4 (bridge with spider scurrying across it): 1, 2, 3, 4, 5, 6, 7, 8, 10, 11.

Level 5 (Nigel the gnome about to eat his breakfast): 1, 2, 3, 5, 6, 7, 8, 10, 11, 12.

FOOTBALL BUBBLE

Egocentric boys tend to write more easily in the first person.

Storytime – editing and publishing

level 2	Paperclip Premiers (PPs)
level 3c/3b	Chosen Champs (CCs)
level 3a/4c	Dream Division (DD)
level 4b/4a+	Longstop Leaguers (LLs)

This lesson follows lessons 12 & 13 and is likely to need longer than the suggested hour.

Game plan

Children will: edit and publish a previously written story.

Training

For children

Make sure the first draft of their story is finished.

For teachers

1 Find a large sheet of sugar paper per child and fold it to make the book cover.
2 Attach to lined paper, cut to size to fit the folded book page size (see page 79 for instructions on how to make a book).
3 Make a book to show children what their finished product will look like.
4 Locate thesauruses and dictionaries.

The match

Warm-up

Ask children to look at *I CAN . . .* target sheets stuck in their books last week. At the bottom of each are **editing targets** – criteria they need to be able to identify and use to achieve their target level.

First half

- Working individually, ask children to read stories from lesson 13, and with a coloured pencil **write improvements** suggested from the *I CAN . . .* targets above. If children have remembered to write on alternate lines, there will be plenty of room for them to do this. If their writing has left no space for this, number lines in the margin, lay a sheet of paper next to the story with numbered lines and write edited improvements in corresponding lines on the sheet.
- Expect children to spend about 15 minutes using dictionaries, thesauruses and *I CAN . . .* targets. Give them space to read their stories out loud.

Half-time PEP talk

Hand out a sheet of sugar paper and **make books** as shown on page 79.

Second half

- Ask children to **copy their story out** – each story part on a different page with the picture gallery in the middle. Insist on really neat presentation and good handwriting. Using separate pieces of paper for each paragraph/part makes copying untidy writing out again easier.
- Blurbs, front covers, ISBN numbers, bar codes, publishing houses and reviews can also be added.

Extra time

- Children should read other children's books.
- Children can write another story using the same five-part structure.

The analysis

Ask children to **share their books and celebrate** their writing achievements.

Shoot-out

These *I CAN . . .* targets may have been achieved:

Low 2 (funny face): 1, 6.

Secure 2 (2 children): 8, 9.

High 2 (penguin on holiday): 6.

Low 3 (trainer): 5.

Secure 3 (twirly flower): 8.

High 3 (cup of tea): 8.

Low 4 (man crawling out of a shark's mouth): 7.

Secure 4 (tiger saying "hello"): 5.

FOOTBALL BUBBLE

Once upon a time, the boys in your class would have been focused hunter-gatherers who didn't waste time on irrelevant activities.

How to make a book

1. Fold a piece of sugar paper into eight.

2. Using scissors, shave off a strip along the fold in the middle two sections.

3. Lay the paper out in landscape and cut along one of the centre folds.

4. Glue the four corner rectangles.

5. Join glued rectangles together to make rigid covers.

6. Rework the folds to make a concertina book.

7. Use the central two pages for a picture gallery. Other pages make a dedication and five story parts.

8. Add a cover and a back blurb.

LESSON **15**

Munich plane crash

level 2	Paperclip Premiers (PPs)
level 3c/3b	Chosen Champs (CCs)
level 3a/4c	Dream Division (DD)
level 4b/4a+	Longstop Leaguers (LLs)

Game plan

Children will: use specific language features and extend vocabulary choices.

Training

For children

Possibly research the Munich plane crash for homework prior to the lesson.

For teachers

1 Eco-copy *What happened on 6 February 1958* on pages 83–84.
2 Photocopy the correct number of *Newspaper article* sheets found on pages 85–88 detailing the Munich plane crash. These can be one between two, except for the PPs who need one each.
3 Locate thesauruses and dictionaries.

The match

Warm-up

Give out *What happened on 6 February 1958* and ask children to **sequence the events** in the grid in the correct order. Write the order number in the column on the right of each box. The correct sequence for all groups is:

	2		4		3
	6		1		5

First half

- In pairs, ask children to **complete the two parts of the second part** of the sheet in their books. For this, PPs will need thesauruses.
- Share answers as a class, writing the **best from each group on the board** to build a bank of phrases and words that include:

  - **Headlines**, e.g. "*Plain Disaster*" or "*Snow Wonder; It Was Plane Obvious.*"
  - **Rhetorical, questions** e.g. *Couldn't they see it was snowing heavily?*
  - **Personification**, e.g. *The sky cried tears while the wind whistled and the snow laughed at the snowploughs.*
  - **Metaphors**, e.g. *A shimmering ball of fire, a sizzling sausage lighting up the sky* or *a toasted marshmallow charred over a fire in the sky.*
  - **Quotes from the Queen**, e.g. *I am very sad to hear about the crash.*
  - **Alliteration**, e.g. *White snow whipped wildly* or *cold, crunchy ice.*
  - **Synonyms** for the word "building," e.g. *house, factory, bungalow, flat.*
  - **Onomatopeias**, e.g. *Aahgch! Shlung!*

  These will be used later in the lesson.

Half-time PEP talk

Ask children to give **verbs** to describe what happened during the crash. Add these to the words on the board, then create actions to describe them. Mime these actions.

Second half

- **Hand out** *Newspaper article*. Ask children to **complete the blanks** as directed in the instructions at the bottom of the page. Some children may need to recap what some of the directed words mean – *e.g. synonyms, similes* – and may need access to dictionaries and thesauruses.
- Encourage children to think of their own ideas as well as the ones on board.

Extra time

Ask children to read through their work again and edit it.

The analysis

Ask children to read their finished pieces of work out to the class and say what they are most pleased with and why.

Shoot-out

Low 2 (funny face): 7.

Secure 2 (2 children): 4.

High 2 (penguin on holiday): 1, 4.

Low 3 (trainer): 1, 4.

Secure 3 (twirly flower): 1, 3, 4, 5.

High 3 (cup of tea): 1, 3, 4.

Secure 4 (tiger saying "hello"): 2, 8.

High 4 (bridge with spider scurrying across it): 1, 2.

Level 5 (Nigel the gnome about to eat his breakfast): 11.

FOOTBALL BUBBLE

Boys' brains are wired to use mostly the left hemisphere for speech. Girls use left and right hemispheres – that's why girls are more adept at conversation.

What happened on 6 February 1958

PPs

On the way home, their plane refuelled at Munich.	The plane skidded on the runway as it took off.	It was snowing. The runway had snow on it.	
Eight of Man United's football team died.	Man United beat Belgrade in the European Cup.	The plane hit a house and burst into flames.	

1 Use a thesaurus to find a synonym for the word **building**.
2 Make up an onomatopoeia to describe a heavy object hitting a house.

What happened on 6 February 1958

CCs

On the way home Manchester United's plane stopped in Munich to refuel.	The aeroplane could not gain enough speed as it sped down the Munich runway.	Snow was falling in Munich. The runway could not be cleared fast enough.	
Twenty-one people died, including eight of Manchester United's talented football team.	Manchester United had beaten Red Star Belgrade in the European Cup.	The plane hit a house near the end of the runway. The front part of the plane burst into flames.	

1 Imagine that the Queen visited your classroom the day after the crash. What might she say?

2 Use alliteration to describe the weather when the plane crashed.

What happened on 6 February 1958

DD

On the way home Manchester United's plane stopped in Munich to refuel.	The aeroplane could not gain enough speed as it sped down the Munich runway.	Snow was falling in Munich. The runway could not be cleared fast enough.	
Twenty-one people died, including eight of Manchester United's talented football team.	Manchester United had beaten Red Star Belgrade in the European Cup.	The plane hit a house near the end of the runway. The front part of the plane burst into flames.	

1 Write a phrase that personifies what the weather was like when the plane crashed.
2 Write a metaphor to describe an aeroplane.

What happened on 6 February 1958

LLs

On the way home Manchester United's plane stopped in Munich to refuel.	The aeroplane could not gain enough speed as it accelerated down the Munich runway.	Snow was falling in Munich. The runway could not be cleared fast enough.	
Twenty-one people died, including eight of Manchester United's talented football team.	Manchester United had beaten Red Star Belgrade in the European Cup.	The plane hit a house near the end of the runway. The front part of the plane burst into flames.	

1 Write a newspaper headline about an aeroplane crash that happened when an aeroplane failed to take off from the runway during a snow storm. This must include a pun. Useful words to play with – plane/plain, weather/whether, crash course.
2 The newspaper report describes what happened. Think of two rhetorical questions that might be included in the article.

Newspaper article

Fill in the gaps. When you come to an underlined number, check what you have to do by looking at the numbers at the bottom of the page.

PPs

Fifty years ago, Manchester United had (1) _____ young players. They beat Red Star Belgrade in the European cup on 6 February 1958 then began to fly home. Their plane stopped at Munich airport in Germany to refuel.

It was snowing as they landed at Munich. The snow was (2) _____ and (2) _____. When the plane tried to take off the aircraft could not get up enough speed. It overshot the runway, and after hitting a house swung to the right, straight into another building.

(3) _____

_____

_____

The front of the plane caught fire. (4) _____

_____

_____

_____

Some players escaped. Of the forty-four people on board, twenty-one died straight away, including the seven Manchester United players. Duncan Edwards, also a player, died in hospital fifteen days later.

1   Another word for talented.
2   Put in an adjective.
3   Describe the crash – what it looked like and what happened inside the plane. Include an onomatopoeia and an adverb.
4   Describe the flames and include alliterative words that all start with the same sound.

Newspaper article

Fill in the gaps. When you come to an underlined number, check what you have to do by looking at the numbers at the bottom of the page.

CCs

In the 1950s, Manchester United's manager, Matt Busby, (1) _____ a squad of talented young players. They flew to Belgrade to play a match in the European Cup. Having beaten Red Star Belgrade on 6 February 1958, they headed back to Manchester via Munich airport in Germany.

It was snowing as they landed at Munich. The snow was like a (2) _____

_____.

When the pilot tried to take off there was so much (3) _____ slush that the aircraft overshot the runway, and after hitting a house swung to the right, straight into another building.

(4) _____

_____

The front of the plane caught fire. (5) _____

_____

Of the forty-two passengers and six crew, twenty-one died instantly including the seven Manchester United players. Duncan Edwards, also a player, died in hospital fifteen days later.

The Queen said how deeply shocked she was by the news. (6) _____

_____

(7) _____

1   Another word for created.
2   Finish the sentence including a simile to describe the weather.
3   Add an adjective.
4   Describe the crash. Include an onomatopoeia and adverb.
5   Describe the flames. Include alliterative words that all start with the same sound.
6   Write something the Queen said using speech marks.
7   Write a rhetorical question people might have asked after the event.

© Heather Butler 2010 *Literacy in Action: Football* Routledge

Newspaper article

When you come to an underlined number, check what you have to do by looking at the numbers at the bottom of the page.

DD

Layout – headline needs to be written in this space.

In the late 1950s, Manchester United's manager, Matt Busby, (1a) _____ a squad of (1b) _____ young players. They played in Belgrade in the European Cup, beating Red Star Belgrade. On 6 February 1958 they flew back to Manchester via Munich airport in Germany where their (2) _____ plane refuelled.

It was snowing in Munich. (3) _____

The plane refuelled and the pilot tried twice to take off. Due to (2) _____ slush on the runway, Captain Thain's aircraft failed to gain enough speed and the plane overshot. After hitting a house it swung to the right, straight into another building. (4) _____

The front of the plane caught fire. (5) _____

_____

Of the thirty-eight passengers and six crew, twenty-one died instantly including seven Manchester United football players. Duncan Edwards, also one of Busby's Babes, died in hospital fifteen days later.

The Queen said how deeply shocked she was by the news. (6) _____

(7) _____

1   Synonyms for . . . (1a) created (1b) talented.
2   Insert an adjective.
3   Describe the weather, including a simile.
4   Make up information to describe the crash – use your five senses to think of imaginative words. Include a metaphor, onomatopoeia and alliteration.
5   Describe the flames. Use alliterative words and personification to say how the flames ripped through the front of the plane (and you cannot use ripped . . .)
6   Write something the Queen said, in speech marks.
7   Write a rhetorical question people might have asked after the event.
8   Now make up a headline for your newspaper article that includes a pun.

Newspaper article

When you come to an underlined number, check what you have to do by looking at the numbers below the text.

LLs

Leave a space to write the headline.

In the late 1950s, Manchester United's manager, Matt Busby, (1a) _____ a squad of (1b) _____ young players. Known as the Busby Babes, they beat Red Star Belgrade in the European Cup. Returning on 6 February 1958, they stopped at Riem Airport in Munich, Germany for their (2) _____ plane to refuel.

It was snowing as their twin-propped plane – called Lord Burghley – landed at Riem. (3) _____.

The plane refuelled and the pilot tried to take off. Due to (2)_____ slush on the runway, Captain James Thain's aircraft failed to gain enough speed for lift-off. (4) _____. On the third trip down the runway the plane overshot, and after hitting a house with its port wing, swung to the right, straight into another building. (5) _____

The front of the plane caught fire. (6) _____

Of the thirty-eight passengers and six crew, twenty-one died instantly including seven Manchester United football players. Duncan Edwards, known as the jewel in the crown of Busby's Babes, died in hospital fifteen days later.

The Queen said how deeply shocked she was by the news. (7) _____.
(8) _____.

1 Synonyms for . . . (1a) created (1b) talented.
2 Insert an adjective.
3 Describe the weather including a simile.
4 Insert a rhetorical question.
5 Make up information to describe the crash – use your five senses to think of imaginative words. Include a metaphor, onomatopoeia and alliteration.
6 Describe the flames. Use alliterative words and also personification to say how the flames ripped through the front of the plane (and you cannot use ripped . . .).
7 Write something the Queen said as a direct quote (these need to be in speech marks). Then write an indirect quote that does not need speech marks. (She later said that . . .).
8 Express an opinion about what happened that night.
9 Now make up a headline for your newspaper article that includes a pun.

FAQs and vocabulary

level 2	**Paperclip Premiers (PPs)**
level 3c/3b	**Chosen Champs (CCs)**
level 3a/4c	**Dream Division (DD)**
level 4b/4a+	**Longstop Leaguers (LLs)**

Game plan

Children will: think about word choices and answer questions as fully as possible for a website.

Training

For children

Bring an object of interest to school AND some information about it.

For teachers

1 Eco-copy *FAQs to answer* on page 92.
2 Find some objects and information for those who forget.
3 Locate thesauruses and dictionaries.

The match

Warm-up

Give children time to **read the information** they have about their object to a partner.

First half

- Ask children to write **adjectives and "technical language"** related to their object in their books.
- Use thesauruses to **find unusual words**. Use dictionaries to check spellings.

Half-time PEP talk

In groups of three or four, ask each child to contribute his or her **longest word**. After each word is said, group members perform a chosen movement jump, skip, hop, etc. for as many syllables as there are in the word. Alternatively, do this as a class activity.

Second half

- The children's **objects are being sold on a website** and the children are going to compile FAQ sheets telling people about them. They must use "technical" words to make people believe they know lots and lots about their object. Model how **full answers** use few pronouns and explain the answer with lots of details. The reader should be able to work out what the question was from the answer.
- Give out *FAQs to answer* to help children begin. If they do not know the exact answer then encourage invented details that are realistic. This is a great skill to develop for story-writing.
- Let PPs answer their questions on the *FAQs to answer* sheet and expect CCs, DDs and LLs to start every answer with a different word. All should include at least one "technical" word per answer – underline these in a coloured pencil – and write sentences of varying lengths that are full and interesting.
- Challenge LLs to give an opinion about their object as well as using a rhetorical question to draw the reader in to want to find out more about the object.
- As answers are for a website, the audience is the general public.
- This task is a good opportunity to complete several *I CAN . . .* targets.

Extra time

- Ask children to think of a name for the website and create further questions and answers.

- They can repeat this process with different objects.

- Ask children to create their own website, including FAQs.

The analysis

In pairs, children should imagine they are writing a **website about themselves**. If they want to, children can imagine they are a famous sports player. Write down **two FAQs** and answers people might want to know.

Shoot-out

These *I CAN* . . . targets may have been achieved this lesson:

Low 2 (funny face): 7.

Secure 2 (2 children): 1, 4, 10.

High 2 (penguin on holiday): 1, 7, 11.

Low 3 (trainer): 3, 4, 6.

Secure 3 (twirly flower): 5, 10c.

Low 4 (man crawling out of a shark's mouth): 1, 4, 5.

Secure 4 (tiger saying "hello"): 2, 6, 12, 13.

High 4 (a bridge with a spider scurrying across it): 4.

Level 5 (Nigel the gnome about to eat his breakfast): 3, 6, 11.

FOOTBALL BUBBLE

In the womb, boys' left brain hemispheres develop later than girls' do. Reasoning and language skills are left-hemisphere activities. Boys have to play catch-up . . .

FAQs to answer

PPs

1   What is your object? _____

2   What is it used for? _____

3   What colours can you buy them in? _____

4   Who uses it? _____

5   Where can I buy a new one? _____

6   Where could it be repaired? _____

FAQs to answer

CCs

1   What is your object?
2   What is it for?
3   What colours can you buy them in?
4   What could I use if I didn't have one?
5   Who would use it?
6   Where can I buy a new one?
7   Where could it be repaired if it breaks?
8   How has the object changed over the last ten years?

FAQs to answer

DD and LLs

1   What is your object?
2   What is it for?
3   What materials is it made of?
4   Who uses it?
5   What would they be doing?
6   What is its expected life span?
7   What is the best feature on this object?
8   Where can I buy a new one?
9   Where could I get it repaired?
10 How has the object changed over the last thirty years?

Connective obituary

level 2	Paperclip Premiers (PPs)
level 3c/3b	Chosen Champs (CCs)
level 3a/4c	Dream Division (DD)
level 4b/4a+	Longstop Leaguers (LLs)

Game plan

Children will: use connectives whilst writing an obituary.

Training

For children

None.

For teachers

1 Photocopy the obituary for *Tiverton Preedy* found on page 96 (where connectives are shown in bold for PPs) and pages 97–99 for everyone else.
2 Possibly bring in an obituary from a newspaper to show the children.

The match

Warm-up

■ In pairs, on whiteboards, ask children to write down as many **connectives and connective phrases** as they can in 2 minutes.
■ Make a list of these on the board and leave them there.

First half

■ Explain what an obituary is and ask children to read the one in memory of *Tiverton Preedy*.
■ Ask them, in pairs, to **fill in the blanks** which are all either straight connectives or connective phrases. Connectives needed are given at the top of each sheet.
■ Quickly work round each group and read through the text letting children tick their answers, some of which could have several correct connectives.

93

Half-time PEP talk

- Look at the list of connectives already on the board and the type of connective each is:

  - linking (*and, but, so*);
  - time (*before, then, after, that*);
  - reason (*because, so*);
  - logical (*however, therefore, although*);
  - clarify (*for example, as shown by, in conclusion, despite this*);
  - a phrase (*earlier on, on the other hand*).

- Some connectives could fit into more than one category, depending on their context.
- Write the above types on the board in a different colour and devise an action for each.
- Now point to connectives. Children **say the connective and perform its action**.

Second half

- Ask children to **write a four-paragraphed obituary** about an imaginary person using as many connectives (and connective phases) as possible. Underline each as they write them. Use the same headings as the modelled obituary for Tiverton Preedy.
- Use this task to create a really good opening sentence, and for LLs a finishing sentence which links to that opening.
- PPs may prefer to draw their character in the middle of the page and write sentences round it.

Extra time

- Ask children to edit obituaries using the edit criteria at the bottom of the *I CAN . . .* sheets.

- They can read obituaries for famous people found on the internet or in newspapers.

- Ask them to write an obituary for someone they have read about, using researched information to complete accurate details.

The analysis

Invite children to **read** their obituary to the class and **count the connectives** as they are used.

Shoot-out

These I CAN . . . targets may have been achieved this lesson:

Low 2 (funny face): 8.

Secure 2 (2 children): 2, 10.

High 2 (penguin on holiday): 2, 9.

Low 3 (trainer): 2, 12.

Secure 3 (twirly flower): 2, 12, 13.

High 3 (cup of tea): 2, 13.

Low 4 (man crawling out of a shark's mouth): 9, 11.

Secure 4 (tiger saying "hello"): 9, 14, 15.

High 4 (bridge with spider scurrying across it): 10, 11.

Level 5 (Nigel the gnome about to eat his breakfast): 4, 12.

FOOTBALL BUBBLE

Male brains have fewer fibres connecting the left and right sides than female brains. This reduces boys' ability to multi-task.

Tiverton Preedy

*Fill in the blanks with **but**, **and**, or **then**. Connectives will need to be used several times.*

PPs

Birth/origin

Tiverton Preedy was born in 1863 in Norfolk _____ went to Bloxham School in Lincolnshire.

Tiverton Preedy's achievements

He trained to be a vicar _____ went to St Peter's church in Barnsley where he helped form a club called Barnsley St Peter's Football Club.

What Preedy's achievements led to

He bought a field for the club _____ charged 2p to watch a match _____ used the money to buy players.

Thanks to Preedy, the club grew _____ was later renamed Barnsley Football Club.

A closing statement

Preedy moved to Islington in London _____ never forgot Barnsley _____ always sent a message to the team if they were playing in a cup match. He died in 1928, a man with a strong Christian faith _____ an amazing leader who will never be forgotten.

Tiverton Preedy

*Fill in the blanks with **and, because, as, then, so** and **although**. Some of the connectives will be used more than once.*

CCs

Birth/origin

Tiverton Preedy was born in Norfolk _____ went to school in Lincolnshire.

Tiverton Preedy's achievements

Tiverton Preedy did not become an estate agent like his father _____ he wanted to be a vicar. After he was ordained* he moved to Barnsley _____ he was asked to be a priest there. Some boys wanted to play football _____ he helped them form Barnsley St Peter's Football Club.

What Preedy's achievements led to

There was nowhere for the club to play _____ Tiverton bought a field _____ charged 2p to people wanting to watch _____ used the money to buy professional players.

_____ he cared about his football team, he also told people about his faith _____ helped people in need. Thanks to him, the club grew _____ was later renamed Barnsley Football Club.

A closing statement

Preedy moved to Islington in London but never forgot Barnsley Football Club _____ they were now called. He died in 1928, a man with a strong Christian faith _____ an amazing leader who will never be forgotten.

* Someone is ordained at a special ceremony in a cathedral before he or she can become a priest or a vicar.

Tiverton Preedy

*Fill in the blanks with **and, but, as, then, so, because, although** and **however**. Some of the connectives will be used more than once.*

DD

Birth/origin

Tiverton Preedy was born in Norfolk _____ he went to Bloxham School in Lincolnshire.

Tiverton Preedy's achievements

He did not become an estate agent like his father _____ went to Lincoln to train to be a vicar. Ordained* in 1888, he moved to Barnsley _____ that he could become a priest there. He also joined a rugby club _____ he hardly played for them _____ there was a match on Good Friday (when Christians remember that Jesus died) _____ Tiverton refused to play on that day for religious reasons.

He met some boys who wanted to play football _____ helped them form a club called Barnsley St Peter's Football Club.

What Preedy's achievements led to

He played for them and _____ a forward scored many goals. Later, he bought a field for the club, charged 2p to watch a match _____ used the money to buy professional players. Thanks to Preedy, the club grew _____ was later renamed Barnsley Football Club.

_____ he cared about his football team, he also told people about his faith _____ helped those in need.

A closing statement

_____ Preedy moved to Islington in London he never forgot Barnsley _____ always sent a message if they were playing in a cup match. He died in 1928, a man of faith _____ an amazing leader who will never be forgotten.

* Someone is ordained at a special ceremony in a cathedral before he or she can become a priest or a vicar.

Tiverton Preedy

*Fill in the blanks with **and, but, as, then, so, because, although, if, when, however, whilst there, later on, contrary to, before long, in order to, that is when, at that time**. Some connectives will be used more than once.*

LLs

Birth/origin

Tiverton Preedy was born on 22 January 1863 in Norfolk _____ went to Bloxham School in Lincolnshire.

Tiverton Preedy's achievements

_____ expectation, when he was aged twenty-two, he did not become an estate agent like his father, _____ went to Lincoln to train to be a vicar. Ordained* in 1888, he moved to St Peter's church in Barnsley _____ become the priest there. _____ he also joined a rugby club. _____, he hardly played for the rugby club _____ there was a match on Good Friday and _____ Christians remember Jesus died. Tiverton Preedy refused to play on that day.

_____ he met some boys who wanted to start a football team __ he helped them form a club called Barnsley St Peter's Football Club. The first meeting was on Tuesday 6 September 1887 _____ Preedy became the financial secretary.

What Preedy's achievements led to

He played for the team and _____ a forward scored many goals. _____ he bought a field for the club and ____ people came to watch charged them 2p _____ used the money to buy professional players.

The club grew _____ changing its name, to Barnsley Football Club.

_____ he cared about his football team, he also told people about his faith _____ helped countless people who were in need.

A closing statement

Preedy moved to Islington in London and _____ he moved he never forgot Barnsley _____ always sent a message if they were playing in a cup match. He died in 1928, a man of strong Christian faith _____ an amazing leader who will never be forgotten.

* Someone is ordained at a special ceremony in a cathedral before he or she can become a priest or a vicar.

Is sport good or bad?

level 2	Paperclip Premiers (PPs)
level 3c/3b	Chosen Champs (CCs)
level 3a/4c	Dream Division (DD)
level 4b/4a+	Longstop Leaguers (LLs)

Game plan

Children will: create a conscience alley and order ideas about whether sport is good or bad.

Training

For children

None.

For teachers

1 Locate thesauruses.
2 Eco-copy *Sport is good/bad* as found on page 103, one between two.
3 Find a symbolic alien.

The match

Warm-up

▩ In pairs, ask children to think of **good and bad things about sport and athletes**:

  ▩ *encourages healthy exercise;*
  ▩ *provides a hobby;*
  ▩ *can be social;*
  ▩ *unifies families;*
  ▩ *provides jobs and identity;*
  ▩ *raises self-esteem;*
  ▩ *creates travel;*
  ▩ *provides good role models;*
▩ **versus**
  ▩ *injuries;*

- *drug scandals;*
- *only one person/team can win;*
- *can be expensive;*
- *is a waste of money and time;*
- *encourages violence;*
- *encourages obsession.*

- Keep ideas as generic as possible and encourage examples from a variety of sports.
- **List these on the board**, in two columns, one for and one against sport.

First half

- Hand out *Sport is good because . . .* In pairs, ask children to **order the three statements** with the one they consider to be the most important as the first. They should copy these in their book (or stick them in with numbers added to clarify the order), then add other statements about why sport is a good thing.
- Repeat with *Sport is bad because . . .*, suggesting the negative aspects of sport.

Half-time PEP talk

- Ask children to take one of the arguments for and against sport and **think of an action to illustrate each one**. This could be done singly or in pairs.
- Stand behind chairs and perform actions.

Second half

- Divide the class in half. Writing children's names on one end of a lollipop stick and drawing the sticks out of a plastic container is a good way to do this fairly. Half will be against sport, half will be for it. They must suspend their own thoughts and feelings for this task. Now divide again into smaller groups of between five and seven. There needs to be the same number of groups for and against.
- In their groups, depending on whether they are designated "for" or "against" sport, they should share their accumulated arguments, choosing a unique argument to be their own. They must practise saying this out loud, all at once.
- Invite one group of pro-sport children to stand in a line with a group of anti-sports opposite, thus making a **conscience alley**. A child holding an alien representative, who knows nothing about sport at all (the alien, not the child), slowly walks down the alley with each child whispering their point as he/she passes by, to persuade the alien to embrace or reject sport.
- The "alien" turns as it reaches the end of the alley and makes a justified decision as to whether it is going to try sport while on Planet Earth.
- Repeat this with other groups to allow every child to experience being part of the alley.
- Ask children to write an article, using paragraphs, for **an alien newspaper** after the alien has returned to its own planet and wants to share his love/hatred of sport with others.
- The article should have a clear opening sentence, put forward both views and let the reader know what the alien really thinks at the end.

Extra time

Ask children to write further articles for the newspaper based on other things the alien engaged with whilst visiting Planet Earth (or your classroom . . .).

The analysis

Ask children to write theirs and other children's **arguments in bullet form** with the most important/persuasive argument first.

Shoot-out

High 2 (trainer): 10.

Low 3 (trainer): 7, 13.

Secure 3 (twirly flower): 6, 13.

High 3 (a cup of tea): 5, 7, 11.

Low 4 (man crawling out of a shark's mouth): 3, 8.

Secure 4 (tiger saying "hello"): 2, 7, 13, 14, 15.

High 4 (bridge with a spider scurrying across it): 3, 10, 11.

Nigel the gnome about to eat his breakfast: 6, 10, 12, 13.

FOOTBALL BUBBLE

Boys tend to perform better when they are asked to repeat the instructions out loud before beginning.

Sport is good because:

- It gives you exercise which keeps you healthy.
- It's good to play as a team.
- It provides jobs.

Sport is good because:

- It gives you exercise which keeps you healthy.
- It's good to play as a team.
- It provides jobs.

Sport is good because:

- It gives you exercise which keeps you healthy.
- It's good to play as a team.
- It provides jobs.

Sport is bad because:

- Athletes are paid too much money.
- There is bad behaviour at matches.
- Athletes provide bad examples of how to behave.

Sport is bad because:

- Athletes are paid too much money.
- There is bad behaviour at matches.
- Athletes provide bad examples of how to behave.

Sport is bad because:

- Athletes are paid too much money.
- There is bad behaviour at matches.
- Athletes provide bad examples of how to behave.

Ixed advert for ladies' football

level 2	Paperclip Premiers (PPs)
level 3c/3b	Chosen Champs (CCs)
level 3a/4c	Dream Division (DD)
level 4b/4a+	Longstop Leaguers (LLs)

Game plan

Children will: include suffixes and prefixes in an advert – suitable for gender curriculum work.

Training

For children

None.

For teachers

1 Eco-copy *Ladies' football* for each group as found on pages 107–108, one between two.
2 Make sure dictionaries are available.

The match

Warm-up

▪ Recap **suffixes** (sad<u>ness</u>, use<u>less</u>, peace<u>ful</u>, comfort<u>able</u>, force<u>fully</u>, football<u>er</u>, thinn<u>est</u>) and **prefixes** (<u>un</u>happy, <u>dis</u>allowed, <u>re</u>organised, <u>mis</u>understood), and create a list of each on the board. Point out that a word with a suffix or prefix always has a smaller word inside it – this is useful for spelling the word correctly.

▪ Find out if children can think of any words that have both (*unusually, irretrievable, uncomfortable*) and make a third list.

▪ Give each of the lists (suffix, prefix, both) a colour code.

First half

■ Hand out *Ladies' football*. In pairs, ask children to carefully read the text (possibly reading and dealing with alternate sentences) and **underline suffixes**, **prefixes** and "**both**" words in the colours decided during the WARM-UP.

■ Check that children have identified suffixes and prefixes correctly.

Half-time PEP talk

Ask children to **instruct the others to do exercises** that last 5 seconds. Instructions must be two words, one a verb and the other a description of that verb that contains either a suffix or prefix. If they use a word with both, everyone must exercise for 10 seconds (*skip carefully, run relentlessly, jump unenthusiastically*).

Second half

■ **Write an advert promoting the original ladies' football team**. The advert's audience is teenage/twenty-year-old girls, and at least two sentences in the advert must be about how ladies' football started (i.e. children must manipulate the information read earlier in the lesson but cannot copy it straight into their books). DDs and LLs should include opinions in their advert, as well as rhetorical questions to make their advert really persuasive.

■ All children are to use as many suffixes and prefixes as possible in the slogans used in their adverts (*be unusual, don't be disorganised, no more sadness on Saturdays, be the fittest, the bolder the better*). Every slogan needs an exclamation mark at the end of it.

Extra time

■ Ask children to use a dictionary to find further words with suffixes, prefixes and words with both.

■ Ask children to create "ixed" word searches.

■ Children should research other sports where women have made an entrance, such as boxing and marathon running. They should write this up, underlining "ixed" words.

■ Ask children to write an advert promoting a different team. This could be ladies', men's or mixed football for any sport. The advert's audience is the age group of the team (think about different age groups – granny, children, teenagers).

The analysis

Swap books with a partner who must read, then underline, all suffix words, prefix words and "both" words using the colour code decided in WARM-UP.

Shoot-out

The following I CAN . . . targets may have been achieved:

Low 2 (funny face): 5.

Secure 2 (2 children): 6a.

High 2 (penguin on holiday): 5a, 11.

Secure 3 (twirly flower): 11.

High 3 (a cup of tea): 3d, 5.

Low 4 (man crawling out of a shark's mouth): 1, 6.

Secure 4 (tiger saying "hello"): 2, 4a, 11.

Level 5 (Nigel the gnome about to eat his breakfast): 6, 11.

FOOTBALL BUBBLE

Girls tend to process emotions more quickly and efficiently than boys. Girls will talk more openly and thus reduce their stress levels. Boys keep hold of their stress until it erupts, often in physical form.

Ladies' football

PPs

In 1894 Nettie Honeywell started an unusual football club.

Thirty young women footballers trained enthusiastically.

They were respectfully called the Northern Women.

Officially the first match was on 23 March 1895.

The disorganised Southern Women lost 7–1.

The rematch was on 6 April 1895.

North London beat the Southerners 8–3.

Daisy Allen, possibly the youngest and fittest player on the pitch, was the star of the match.

Ladies' football

CCs

In 1894 Nettie Honeywell put an unusual advert in the newspaper. She wished to start a British ladies' football club. J. W. Julian, who played for Tottenham Hotspurs, became coach to the thirty young women who signed up. They improved their fitness by training at Alexandra Park Racecourse and were known as the Northern Women's team. Officially the first match was on 23 March 1895. Unhappily for the Southern Women, they were useless and disorganised and lost 7–1.

The rematch was on 6 April 1895 in Brighton. North London beat the Southerners 8–3. Daisy Allen, the North's left-winger and possibly the youngest and fittest player on the pitch, was the star of the match.

Ladies' football

DD and LLs

In 1894, Nettie Honeywell placed an unusual advert in the newspapers. She intentionally set out to annoy people by saying she wished to start a British ladies' football club. Lady Florence Dixie offered to become president of the club. J. W. Julian, who played for Tottenham Hotspurs, happily agreed to coach the thirty young women who signed up. Twice weekly they enthusiastically trained at Alexandra Park Racecourse in Hornsey.

Officially the first match was at Crouch End in London on 23 March 1895. The women from North London beat the useless and disorganised Southern Women 7–1. A newspaper reporter watched and claimed the losing team was wandering aimlessly and ungracefully over the pitch.

After this match the British Ladies' Football Club was unstoppable, and on 6 April 1895 played again, this time in Brighton, raising money for medical charities. North London beat the Southerners 8–3. Daisy Allen, the North's left-winger and possibly the youngest on the pitch, was the star of the match.

Ladies' football

DD and LLs

In 1894, Nettie Honeywell placed an unusual advert in the newspapers. She intentionally set out to annoy people by saying she wished to start a British ladies' football club. Lady Florence Dixie offered to become president of the club. J. W. Julian, who played for Tottenham Hotspurs, happily agreed to coach the thirty young women who signed up. Twice weekly they enthusiastically trained at Alexandra Park Racecourse in Hornsey.

Officially the first match was at Crouch End in London on 23 March 1895. The women from North London beat the useless and disorganised Southern Women 7–1. A newspaper reporter watched and claimed the losing team was wandering aimlessly and ungracefully over the pitch.

After this match the British Ladies' Football Club was unstoppable, and on 6 April 1895 played again, this time in Brighton, raising money for medical charities. North London beat the Southerners 8–3. Daisy Allen, the North's left-winger and possibly the youngest on the pitch, was the star of the match.

LESSON **20**

Wheelchair football in a sentence

level 2	Paperclip Premiers (PPs)
level 3c/3b	Chosen Champs (CCs)
level 3a/4c	Dream Division (DD)
level 4b/4a+	Longstop Leaguers (LLs)

Game plan

Children will: focus on clauses and sentence construction, including complex sentences, for a newspaper article – suitable for work exploring issues disabled people face.

Training

For children

None.

For teachers

1 Eco-copy *Wheelchair football* on page 112, enough for one between two.
2 Write the following four sentences on the board before the lesson begins . . .

> *Goal!*
> *Wheelchair football matches last for 40 minutes.*
> *Only two players from the defending team are allowed to enter the penalty area and push-ins replace throw-ins.*
> *Four players, with specially adapted wheelchairs, play together on one team.*

The match

Warm-up

■ **Discuss the sentence types** on the board and make sure children understand the definitions.

  ■ *One-word sentences – tell the reader something using just one word.*
  ■ *Simple sentences – have three parts: a subject, an object and a verb.*

■ *Compound sentences – are two smaller sentences joined by a connective. The connective could be taken out and each of the two sentences would still make sense separately.*

■ *Complex sentences – are clauses joined together by connectives or commas, but each clause would not make sense on its own.*

First half

■ Look at the information given on *Wheelchair football* in note form. On their whiteboards, ask children to write several sentences about it. Expect PPs and CCs to use simple and compound sentences, and DD and LLs to use complex sentences as well.

■ Ask children to share and check these with a partner.

Half-time PEP talk

Read out the following sentences and ask children to **decide which type** of sentence each is. Hold up one arm for one-word sentences, two arms for simple sentences, stand up for compound sentences and stand up and balance on one leg for complex sentences. Alternatively do something that includes moving less vigorously.

■ *Wheelchair football is a sport.* (simple)

■ *Wheelchair football, with its national football league, is played on a five-a-side pitch.* (complex)

■ *Shoot!* (one-word)

■ *There are four players on each side and there are also four subs.* (compound)

■ *Wheelchair football uses a 33 cm football.* (simple)

■ *Run!* (one-word)

■ *The goal mouth is 6 m wide.* (simple)

■ *Players use wheelchairs known as powerchairs to move round the pitch.* (complex)

Second half

In pairs, ask children to write a **newspaper article** explaining what wheelchair football is. Remind children to use good connectives. Before they start writing, check on their *I CAN . . .* targets to see which ones they should try to include.

Extra time

■ Ask children to imagine they are a wheelchair footballer and write an account of a match they played in. Make sure all sentence types are used.

■ Research other disabled sporting activities such as the Paralympics and write further articles about them.

The analysis

- As children read their work, **identify which type of sentence has been used** and underline each type in a different colour with a key at the top of the page to link colours and sentences.
- Check a friend's writing and write a comment about how well he/she had done.

Shoot-out

These *I CAN* . . . targets may have been achieved during this lesson:

Low 2 (funny face): 8.

Secure 2 (2 children): 1, 2.

Low 3 (trainer): 2.

Secure 3 (twirly flower): 2.

High 3 (cup of tea): 2.

Low 4 (man crawling out of a shark's mouth): 2, 9.

Secure 4 (tiger saying "hello"): 9, 10.

High 4 (bridge with a spider scurrying across it): 6.

Level 5 (Nigel the gnome about to eat his breakfast): 2.

FOOTBALL BUBBLE

Boys tend to be better at spatial relationships than girls.

Wheelchair football

- Played indoors.
- Five-a-side pitch.
- Goals – 6m wide.
- 33cm football.
- Four players play at any one time.
- Four subs per team.
- Powerchairs are specially adapted.
- Two halves of 20 minutes each.
- Throw-ins are push-ins.
- Two players only from defending team can enter penalty area.
- One defender only to tackle someone else.
- 2007 – Wheelchair Football Association started a national football league.

Wheelchair football

- Played indoors.
- Five-a-side pitch.
- Goals – 6m wide.
- 33cm football.
- Four players play at any one time.
- Four subs per team.
- Powerchairs are specially adapted.
- Two halves of 20 minutes each.
- Throw-ins are push-ins.
- Two players only from defending team can enter penalty area.
- One defender only to tackle someone else.
- 2007 – Wheelchair Football Association started a national football league.

Five-sense poems

level 2	Paperclip Premiers (PPs)
level 3c/3b	Chosen Champs (CCs)
level 3a/4c	Dream Division (DD)
level 4b/4a+	Longstop Leaguers (LLs)

Game plan

Children will: write and publish a short poem based on the five senses.

Training

For children

None.

For teachers

1 Photocopy appropriate *Footie poem* scaffolds on pages 116–122, one per child.
2 Write the following words on the board before the lesson begins . . .

- PP – *heir, hear, see.*
- CC – *pair, bare, new, dye, to (two other words).*
- DD – *feat, ate, stair, their (two other words).*
- LL – *grate, reign (two other words), write (two other words), male.*

The match

Warm-up

Working in pairs, ask children to **write different words that sound the same** in their books, using the words on the board as a starting point. Which group is to do which words is indicated at the beginning of each line (*2 other words* relates only to the word immediately preceding it).

First half

- Hand out *Footie poem*. Children are to write **a scaffolded poem based on the five senses**. Ask children to read through what they are to include with a partner and briefly discuss what they could write as the first couple of boxes.
- Children should complete the boxes on the left of the grid. What to write is given on the right.
- If children would prefer to write about a match that is not a football one, encourage them to do so.

Half-time PEP talk

- **Reinforce the there/their/they're homophone**. Write the following sentence on the board:

    They're over there with their boots!

- As there are three words that are homophones, children must stand up and jump up and down (or something equally energetic) three times.
- Ask children to think of other homophone sentences and repeat exercise as appropriate.

Second half

- Ask children to remain standing, pick up their books and **read their poems out loud, all together**. This is to help them find out if lines are the right length, have a rhythm and read easily.
- Ask them to sit down and **edit poems using the criteria at the bottom of *Footie poem***.
- Any child who has already used or who can edit a homophone into their poem can be applauded.

Extra time

- Children should reread their poems and add extra lines for each of the five senses.

- Ask them to write sentences using homophones and homonyms. Copy these out for the special words using bubble writing.

The analysis

Ask children to **copy the poem out** taking great care with handwriting and presentation.

Shoot-out

Low 2 (funny face): 1, 3, 4, 6.

Secure 2 (2 children): 5, 8, 9.

High 2 (penguin on holiday): 1, 3, 6.

Low 3 (trainer): 1, 5, 8.

Secure 3 (twirly flower): 4, 5, 7, 8.

High 3 (cup of tea): 3, 4, 8.

Low 4 (man crawling out of a shark's mouth): 7.

Secure 4 (tiger saying "hello"): 4, 5.

High 4 (a bridge with a spider scurrying across it): 1, 2, 9.

Level 5 (Nigel the gnome about to eat his breakfast): 7, 11.

FOOTBALL BUBBLE

Girls have larger memory storage capacity for random information. Boys can be helped to remember better if information is presented in a logical, organised way.

Footie poem

PPs

I go to a football match	
	who you go with
I look and I see	
	colours you see at a match
	describe an object you can see
I listen and I hear	
	a sound you hear at the match
	what it reminds you of
I sniff and I smell	
	write something you can smell
	what it is like
I lick my lips and I taste	
	what you eat at half-time
	what you drink afterwards
I lift my arms and cheer	
	why you lift your arms and cheer
	what you say to the person you are with
The match is over	
	how you feel as you travel home

NOW . . .

- Read your work to check that it makes sense.
- Are all your capital letters right?
- Have you spelt every word correctly?

WHEN YOU PUBLISH YOUR POEM . . .

- Make sure all your letters start and stop in the right places.
- Every **g**, **p**, **j**, **q** and **y** must sit on the line.
- All **t**, **l**, **k**, **f**, **b** and **d** letters must be taller than the others.

Footie poem

CCs

I go to a football match	synonym for go (use a thesaurus)
	who you go with
	it is a special occasion – why are you there?
I look and I see	synonym for look (use a thesaurus)
	something you see on the pitch
	describe it using a simile
I listen and I hear	
	the loudest sound you hear at the match
	what it makes you feel inside
I sniff and I smell	
	describe something you smell
	how close is it – has it travelled a long way?
I lick my lips and I taste	
	what you eat at half-time
	describe it using a metaphor
I lift my arms and cheer	
	why you lift your arms and cheer
	why what has happened is important
The match is over	
	how you feel as you leave the sports venue
	what you say to the person who brought you to the match

continued

NOW . . .

- Check you have put "" in the last sentence.
- Are all your verbs in the right tense? This poem happens today.
- Are full stops and capital letters in the right places?
- Do all your spellings look right? Check them if they don't.

WHEN YOU PUBLISH YOUR POEM . . .

Make sure all your letters are joined up correctly.

Footie poem

DD

I go to a football match	synonym for go (use a thesaurus)
	your relationship with the people you are with
	it is a special occasion – why are you there?
I look and I see	synonym for see (use a thesaurus)
	something you see in the distance
	describe it using a simile
I listen and I hear	
	something someone says to you
And that makes me feel like a . . .	describe what you feel like using a simile
I sniff and I smell	synonym for sniff (use a thesaurus)
	describe something unusual you can smell
	write a rhetorical question about it
I lick my lips and I taste	find a synonym for lick and taste (use a thesaurus)
	what you eat at half-time and who buys it for you
	describe the food using a metaphor
I lift my arms and cheer	
	why you lift your arms and cheer
	what everyone around you is doing
The match is over	
	what you think as you leave

continued

NOW . . .

■ Check you have put "" round speech and? after questions.
■ Is every spelling correct?
■ Are there any adjectives or adverbs you could add?

WHEN YOU PUBLISH YOUR POEM . . .

Make sure all your letters join up.

Footie poem

LLs

I go to a football match	synonym for go (use a thesaurus)
	your relationship with the people you are with
	it was a special occasion – why are you there?
I look and I see	synonym for look and see (use a thesaurus)
	something you see surprises you
	describe it using a metaphor
I listen and I hear	synonym for listen and hear (use a thesaurus)
	you hear something you don't like
	why you don't like it
I sniff and I smell	synonym for sniff (use a thesaurus)
	describe something unusual you smell
	write a rhetorical question about the smell
I lick my lips and I taste	find a synonym for taste (use a thesaurus)
	what you ate and drank at half-time
	how is it different from last time you were at a match?
I lift my arms and cheer	synonym for cheer (use a thesaurus)
	why you lift your arms and cheer
	what others in the stadium are doing
The match is over	
	what your first thought is as the match ends
	tie your last line up with the beginning – include who you are with or the special occasion you have come to the match for

continued

NOW . . .

- Check at least three spellings in the dictionary.
- Can punctuation add anything to the poem?
- Does your rhetorical question draw the reader into the poem?
- Is every single word the best one? Find a place to repeat one for effect.

WHEN YOU PUBLISH YOUR POEM . . .

Make sure your poem is beautifully presented.

Playing with words and boots

level 2	Paperclip Premiers (PPs)
level 3c/3b	Chosen Champs (CCs)
level 3a/4c	Dream Division (DD)
level 4b/4a+	Longstop Leaguers (LLs)

Game plan

Children will: use technical words and homonyms, find small words inside longer ones and create a wordsearch.

Training

For children

None.

For teachers

1 Photocopy the information about *Football boots* on pages 126–129 one each.
2 Eco-copy *Wordsearch*, enough to share one between two – see page 130.
3 Have dictionaries available for children to use.
4 Large squared paper for a wordsearch.

The match

Warm-up

- Hand out and in pairs **read the details** about *Football Boots*.
- Ask children to take a coloured pencil and neatly underline any words they think are technical/specific to boots. Ignore words in italics, bold or underlined. They are for later in the lesson.

First half

- Go through the text again, this time **writing down small words** that are inside larger ones. Each sheet has foot**ball**ers and l**eat**her on the top line as an example.

- In their books, children should write the longer word first, then any smaller words. "Footballers" has *foot*, *ball*, *all*, but not tall as the letter *b* gets in the way.
- Emphasise that looking for small words inside longer ones can help with spelling.
- Now look at **homonyms**. Each sheet has examples of these underlined. Model sentences with the words *iron* and *long* in (all groups use these words), showing the two meanings even though the words are spelt the same. Then ask children to find other words, and write two sentences in their books for each word.

  - PP and CC – ball.
  - DD – down, feel.
  - LL – state, pitch.

Half-time PEP talk

Recap the difference between **verbs and adverbs** and write some on the board – *jump wildly*, *sing sweetly*, *run (on the spot) quickly*, *sleep loudly*. Ask children to think of a few more, then act them out.

Second half

- In italics and underlined are words that belong to **families** that sound the same apart from the first letter/blend sound. Ask children to find their italicised words and add as many words as they can think of to make a family. Use dictionaries to help accurate spelling. For example, leather, feather and heather are in the same family.

  - PP – not, fill, that.
  - CC – feet, that, fast.
  - DD – nails, stand, give.
  - LL – leather, bought, synthetic.

- Ask children to make a **wordsearch** using words from their given text (as well as others). Hand out *Wordsearch*, hand out squared paper and look at the rules together and make sure everyone understands how a wordsearch works.

Extra time

- Ask children to search the text for homophones – some have already been underlined and italicised in the text – and underline them using a coloured pencil.
- They can repeat the word play from this lesson with other texts.

The analysis

Count up the scores from the wordseaches and swap with a partner to check that spellings are 100% accurate.

Shoot-out

These *I CAN* . . . targets may have been achieved:

Low 2 (funny face): 4, 5.

Secure 2 (2 children): 7.

High 2 (penguin on holiday): 7.

Low 3 (trainer): 10, 11.

Secure 3 (twirly flower): 11.

Secure 4 (tiger saying "hello"): 12.

FOOTBALL BUBBLE

Girls have a more highly developed awareness of speech and can process grammatical structures and produce words more effectively than boys.

Football boots

PP

1 Origin

In the beginning . . . Footballers wore the leather boots they owned because they needed strong boots to protect their feet and ankles.

2 Next

Safety measures . . . Rule 13 was set in 1863 saying that no one wearing nails or <u>iron</u> plates on the bottom of his boots could play.

Studs . . . These were first used in 1886 and could *not* be more than half an inch.

Boots especially for football . . . By 1888, thick, heavyweight leather boots were made especially for football.

Players would *fill* the bath with hot water and put their boots on. Then they stood for a <u>long</u> time in the water until the leather fitted itself to the player's foot.

3 Then

Choice . . . Some boots are made of material *that* is not leather because this makes them cheaper and lighter. Studs are made of plastic or metal and players choose which is best after looking at the weather and the pitch.

Players say they prefer to feel the <u>ball</u> than have the protection heavy leather boots give.

Football boots

CC

1 Origin

In the beginning . . . Footballers wore any leather boots they owned to protect their *feet* and ankles. Some players nailed extra bits of leather to their soles to give them a better <u>grip</u>.

2 Next

Safety measures . . . In 1863, Rule 13 said no nails or <u>iron</u> plates on the bottom of boots were allowed.

Studs . . . These were first used in 1886.

Boots especially for football . . . By 1888, thick, heavyweight leather boots were being made especially for football.

Players would buy boots *that* were a tight fit, take them home, fill the bath with hot water, put their boots on and stand for a <u>long</u> time in the water until the boots moulded round their feet to give a tight fit.

3 Then

Lighter-weight boots . . . These appeared in the mid 1950s.

Choice . . . Football boots had screw-in studs made of rubber or plastic. Players could choose which studs they used depending on the weather. Some boots are made of material that is not leather. These are cheaper and lighter.

Adapting to a change of playing style . . . Modern football is about kicking, controlling the <u>ball</u> and moving *fast*. Players say they prefer to feel the ball rather than have the protection heavy leather boots give.

Football boots

DD

1 Origin

In the beginning . . . Footballers wore any leather boots they owned to protect their feet and ankles. Some players nailed extra bits of leather to their soles as this gave a better grip.

2 Next

Safety measures . . . In 1863, Rule 13 was introduced by the Football Association. There were to be no projecting *nails* or <u>iron</u> plates on the soles of boots.

Studs . . . In 1891 the Football Association allowed football boots fitted with leather studs as <u>long</u> as they weren't longer than half an inch. Studs had first been introduced in 1886.

Boots especially for football . . . By 1888 thick, heavyweight leather boots were being made especially for football, with hardened leather for the toe.

Players would buy boots that were tight, take them home, fill the bath with hot water, put their boots on and *stand* for a long time in the water until the boots moulded round their feet to give a tight fit.

3 Then

Lighter-weight boots . . . These appeared in the mid 1950s.

Choice . . . Football boots had screw-in studs made of rubber or plastic. Players would choose which studs they used depending on the weather.

Leather boots stretch out of shape in wet conditions. Synthetic boots are cheaper and lighter and laces now often run <u>down</u> the side of the boot which creates a bigger, flatter area to control and strike the ball.

Adapting to a change of playing style . . . Modern football is about kicking, controlling the ball and moving fast. Players say they prefer to <u>feel</u> the ball rather than have the protection heavy leather boots *give*.

Football boots

LL

1 Origin

In the beginning . . . Footballers wore any leather boots they owned to protect their feet and ankles. Some players nailed extra bits of *leather* to their soles as this gave a better grip.

2 Next

Safety measures . . . In 1863, Rule 13 was introduced by the Football Association. No one was allowed to wear projecting nails, <u>iron</u> plates or gutta percha* on the soles of boots.

Introduction of studs . . . In 1891 the Football Association allowed football boots fitted with studs if they were made of leather. Studs had first been introduced in 1886.

Boots especially for football . . . By 1888 boots were being manufactured especially for football. They were made of thick, heavyweight leather with hardened leather for the toe (players toe-kicked the ball).

Boots were always *bought* slightly small. Players would fill the bath with hot water, put their boots on and stand for a <u>long</u> time in the water until the boots moulded round their feet. This gave them a tight fit.

3 Then

Lighter-weight boots . . . These appeared in the mid 1950s.

Choice . . . Football boots had screw-in studs made of rubber or plastic, and players would choose which studs they used depending on the weather and the <u>state</u> of the <u>pitch</u>.

Leather boots fit well round a player's foot and stretch out of shape in wet conditions. *Synthetic* boots are cheaper and lighter and now often have laces down the side which creates a bigger, flatter area to control and strike the ball.

Adapting to a change of playing style . . . Modern football is about kicking, controlling the ball and moving fast. Nowadays players tend to use their insteps and not their toes to kick the ball, so boots have changed to suit this. The ankle is now exposed and the toe cap has softened. Players say they prefer to feel the ball rather than have the protection heavy leather boots give.

* gutta percha is a whitish rubbery substance taken from trees grown in Malaysia. It's sometimes used nowadays by dentists in root fillings.

Wordsearch

- The first letter of every word must be written in green so it can be found.

- Words can read vertically, horizontally or diagonally but must be in a straight line.

- Every word spelt correctly scores 1 point. If there are smaller words inside a long word then score an extra point for every word inside.

- Record every wordsearch word in your books like this . . .
  Football (3) football, foot, ball, all. The number in brackets shows how many smaller words there are inside the bigger one. These will be counted up at the end to score.

- All words must be three letters or longer.

- Any word that is a homonym scores 2 extra points. Underline it as you write it down.

Wordsearch

- The first letter of every word must be written in green so it can be found.

- Words can read vertically, horizontally or diagonally but must be in a straight line.

- Every word spelt correctly scores 1 point. If there are smaller words inside a long word then score an extra point for every word inside.

- Record every wordsearch word in your books like this . . .
  Football (3) football, foot, ball, all. The number in brackets shows how many smaller words there are inside the bigger one. These will be counted up at the end to score.

- All words must be three letters or longer.

- Any word that is a homonym scores 2 extra points. Underline it as you write it down.

Match report

Game plan

Children will: write match reports in different genres.

Training

For children

None.

For teachers

1 Photocopy (one between two) *Write a report* as found on pages 134–135.

The match

Warm-up

Using four columns, write **genre types** – COMEDY, HORROR, ROMANTIC and FAIRY STORY – on the board. Ask children to contribute to a communal list of what makes each genre unique. Keep a gap along the bottom of the list for key features of report-writing to be written down.

- *COMEDY – quirky characters, slapstick, plays on weaknesses, black comedy makes something funny that normally isn't.*
- *HORROR – concentrates on mood and atmosphere with unexpected things happening all the time, characters do scary things (often on their own), vampires, ghosts, forests, castles, lightning, graveyards, deserted buildings, high drama and suspense, things that are normal become scary, plays on what the reader is scared of, five senses are used in description (shadows, cobwebs, wild screams).*
- *ROMANTIC – usually written for girls and women, narrative moves very fast, characters' thoughts and feelings are often written down, slushy love stories, colour pink, red roses, kisses, catching someone's eye across a crowded room.*

FAIRY STORY – once upon a time . . ., and they all lived happily ever after, easy language, often includes a journey, repetition, talking animals, wishes, spells, princes, princesses, frogs, wicked witches, fairy godmothers, woods, castles, cottages, names often tell the reader what the person is like, people are good or bad, good defeats evil, things happen in threes, extreme conditions such as bright and sunny or dark and gruesome.

First half

- Recap key features of **report-writing** – *definite purpose and audience, successive paragraphs sequence events, use of connective phrases and words such as after that . . . next . . . immediately after . . ., written in the past tense and can include an opinion (in which case it becomes a biased report).*
- Using a different colour to the four genre features, make a list of these on the board for children to refer to later on.

Half-time PEP talk

Ask children to create **frozen statues** suitable to represent different genres. Other children have to guess what the genre is. Use the four above but also encourage children to think of others and their unique qualities.

Second half

- Highlight the need for a strong opening sentence and closing statement.
- Now choose one of two genres and following the given scaffold, **complete a report** for the given audience.

Extra time

- Ask children to write a further report using a different genre style.

- Ask children to write a report switching genres halfway through and see if friends can identify which two genres have been used.

The analysis

- Ask children to read through reports looking for at least two places to **edit and improve**. Check the *I CAN . . .* edit targets to help this.
- Invite children to read their report out and the others children to guess the genre.

Shoot-out

I CAN . . . targets that may have been achieved this lesson are:

Low 2c (funny face): 1, 2, 3, 4, 7, 8.

Secure 2 (2 children): 1, 2, 3, 4, 5, 6, 10.

High 2 (penguin on holiday): 1, 2, 3, 4, 5, 7, 8, 9, 10, 11.

Low 3 (trainer): 2, 3, 4, 7, 8, 9, 13.

Secure 3 (twirly flower): 1, 2, 3, 5, 6, 10, 13.

High 3 (cup of tea): 1, 2, 3, 4, 5, 6, 7, 10, 11.

Low 4 (man crawling out of a shark's mouth): 1, 2, 3, 4, 6, 8, 9, 10, 11.

Secure 4 (tiger saying "hello"): 2, 4, 7, 8b, 9, 10, 11, 12, 13, 14. 15, 16, 17.

High 4 (bridge with a spider scurrying across it): 1, 2, 3, 5, 6, 7, 8, 10, 11.

Level 5 (Nigel the gnome about to eat his breakfast): 1, 2, 3, 4, 5, 6, 10, 11, 12, 13.

FOOTBALL BUBBLE

Girls can sometimes process too much emotive material and become personally involved, losing objectivity.

Write a report

PPs and CCs choose from:

Audience – Clowns Football (or other sport) Club podcast

Genre – comedy

- Which two teams were playing?
- Who took the first ball?
- What happened when a player took the penalty in this match?
- What did he do after he scored the goal?
- How did he get injured?
- What was quirky and funny about the substitute?
- What did the crowd do?
- What is the final score?
- Who was the man/woman of the match?

Audience – readers of www.spookymatches.com

Genre – horror

- Where was the match taking place?
- Which two teams were playing?
- What was the weather like?
- Who was watching in the crowd?
- What was scary about the referee?
- What was his name?
- What was happening to the players during the first half?
- Who scored the first goal?
- What happened to the scorer?
- Who takes it and what was the atmosphere in the stadium like?
- Why was a penalty given?
- Who was injured and how?
- What was scary about the substitute?
- Who was the man/woman of the match?

Write a report

DDs and LLs

Audience – news report on Go Girls radio station

Genre – romantic

- Make sure your introduction is a good one . . .
- Where was the match taking place?
- Which two teams were playing?
- Who was the player in number 8 shirt?
- What did he look like?
- How did the crowd react to him?
- Who scored the first goal?
- How did the scorer react?
- Who took the penalty?
- What was the atmosphere in the stadium like?
- Who was injured and how?
- What did the crowd do when the substitute came on?
- Who was the man/woman of the match?
- Add a closing statement that includes your opinions about the match.

Audience – Fairy Land's leading newspaper's sports pages

Genre – fairy tale

- Think of fairy tale words to open your report . . .
- Where was the match taking place?
- Which two teams were playing?
- Who were the leading players on each side?
- What were their names?
- What happened when each of the three goals were scored?
- What was the atmosphere in the stadium like?
- Who was injured and how?
- What did the crowd do when the substitute came on?
- Who was the man/woman of the match?
- Add a closing statement that includes your opinions about the match.

Commas, clauses and café menus

level 2	Paperclip Premiers (PPs)
level 3c/3b	Chosen Champs (CCs)
level 3a/4c	Dream Division (DD)
level 4b/4a+	Longstop Leaguers (LLs)

Game plan

Children will: use commas and clauses to create a café menu.

Training

For children

None.

For teachers

1 Eco-copy the information about *Fish and chips* on pages 139–142, one per child.

The match

Warm-up

- Write the following list of things that happen to a teacher during a school day on the board. Write without **commas** or the final "and" – e.g. *marking staff meeting children coming in class teaching*.
- Now put commas in the wrong places – e.g. *marking staff, meeting children, coming in, class teaching* – and talk about what each set of two words could mean. Point out that there is nothing to show that the list is nearly ended – i.e. the importance of the word *and*. (There is also the possibility of marking colleagues on how well they meet children.)
- Now move the commas to their correct place – e.g. *marking, staff meeting, children coming in class* and *teaching*.
- Ask children to **create a list of their favourite things** (sports teams, pop stars, colours, days of the week, places) and include commas and the final *and*.

First half

- Commas are also important to mark when an extra piece of information, or **clause**, has been dropped into the sentence. Write an example on the board – *Fish and chips, a family favourite*, is often sold at matches. Underline the piece of extra information that the dropped-in clause has given.
- Hand out the information about *Fish and chips* and ask children to **mark on the punctuation**. To help them do this, read their sentences out several times (to become familiar with vocabulary), then notice where they pause for natural comma spaces.
- LLs must also mark where new paragraphs should start.

Half-time PEP talk

Standing behind their chairs, **chant the following** . . .

We are great at writing, (jump up and down and shout "yahoo!")
What we write is brill (thumbs-up sign)
We paint pictures using words (be artists)
And now we will be still. (sit down)

Second half

- A new sports café is opening up near a sports stadium. Children are to create the menu using commas and dropped-in clauses, as outlined on each group's *Fish and chips* sheet.
- PPs are to write a straight menu with its ingredients listed.

Extra time

- Children can add further dishes with names that reflect different sports.
- Children can copy out and decorate the menus.

The analysis

Hold a **conversation** about what children will do at lunchtime using "dropped clauses" and lists in every sentence.

137

Shoot-out

I CAN . . . targets that might have been achieved this lesson are:

Secure 2 (2 children): 6b.

High 2 (penguin on holiday): 5b.

Low 3 (trainer): 9.

High 3 (cup of tea): 3b.

Low 4 (man crawling out of a shark's mouth): 2.

Secure 4 (tiger saying "hello"): 4c.

High 4 (bridge with a spider scurrying across it): 6a.

Level 5 (Nigel the gnome about to eat his breakfast): 2, 4.

FOOTBALL BUBBLE

Boys respond better if given short, focused writing tasks.

Fish and chips

PPs

Add the commas.

■ Chips or "pommes de terre frites" as they were called are said to have been invented in France.

■ Chips which first appeared in Europe 425 years ago are made from potatoes.

■ Fried fish was served in Lancashire London Hull Manchester Cardiff and Glasgow.

■ In 1995 over 300,000,000 that's 300 million servings of fish and chips were eaten in the UK.

■ Fish and chips are often eaten with beans peas salad or sweetcorn.

Write the menu for The New Sports Café. Here are some ideas to help you begin:

■ *Fish fingers, peas, carrots and chips.*
■ *Chicken, green beans, rice and white sauce.*

Fish and chips

CCs

Add the commas and full stops.

Chips or "pommes de terre frites" as they were called are said to have been invented by the French Chips which first appeared in Europe 425 years ago are made from potatoes

One hundred and sixty years ago in East London fish was being fried and sold as a takeaway meal A famous writer called Charles Dickens wrote about it in his book Oliver Twist Fried fish was served in Lancashire and London Before long places like Hull Manchester Cardiff and Glasgow were selling it too

In 1995 over 300,000,000 – that's 300 million – servings of fish and chips were eaten in the UK They are often eaten with beans peas salad or sweetcorn

- **Write the menu for The New Sports Café.**
- **The name of each dish should be about a sport.**
- **Here are some ideas to help you begin:**

  - *Fish Finger Backstroke – fish fingers, peas, carrots and chips.*
  - *Chicken Goal Scorer – chicken, green beans, rice and white sauce.*

Fish and chips

DD

Add commas, full stops and change some letters to capitals.

chips or "pommes de terre frites" as they were called are said to have been invented by the french made from potatoes which were thought to have been discovered by the explorer sir walter raleigh chips were served with fried fish 160 years ago in East London they were sold as a takeaway meal a writer called charles dickens wrote about it in his book oliver twist

fried fish was served in lancashire and london first before long places like hull manchester cardiff and glasgow were selling them too in 1995 over 300,000,000 – that's 300 million – servings of fish and chips were eaten in the UK often with beans peas salad or sweetcorn

■ **Write details about the menu for The New Sports Café.**
■ **Each item must have a clause dropped in giving extra information about the dish. The name of each dish should be about a sport.**
■ **Here are some ideas to help you begin . . .**

    ■ *Fish Finger Backstroke – fish fingers, lightly grilled by our wonderful chef, peas, carrots and chips.*
    ■ *Chicken Goal Scorer – chicken, slowly roasted over a charcoal bar be cue, green beans, rice and white sauce.*

PHOTOCOPIABLE RESOURCE

Fish and chips

LLs

Add commas, full stops, capital letters and mark where new paragraphs should start.

chips or frites' pommes de terre are said to have been as they were called invented by the French made from potatoes which were thought to have been discovered by the explorer sir walter raleigh 425 years before chips were served with fried fish 160 years ago in East London they were sold as a takeaway meal a famous writer called charles dickens wrote about it in his book oliver twist fried fish was first served in lancashire and london before long places like hull manchester cardiff and glasgow were selling them too in 1995 over 300,000,000 – that's 300 million servings of fish and chips were eaten in the UK often with beans peas salad or sweetcorn

- Write a description, using paragraphs, about different dishes on the menu at The New Sports Café.
- Each item described must have a clause dropped in giving extra information about the dish.
- The name of each dish should be about a sport.
- See how many different connectives can be used to help move from one idea to another.

First there is the Fish Finger Backstroke which comprises four fish fingers, lightly grilled by our wonderful chef, peas, carrots and chips. This is bound to be popular with younger visitors to the café.

List of levels

- ◼ Low 2 (funny face)

- ◼ Secure 2 (2 children)

- ◼ High 2 (penguin on holiday)

- ◼ Low 3 (trainer)

- ◼ Secure 3 (twirly flower)

- ◼ High 3 (cup of tea)

- ◼ Low 4 (man crawling out of a shark's mouth)

- ◼ Secure 4 (tiger saying "hello")

- ◼ High 4 (bridge with a spider scurrying across it)

- ◼ Level 5 (Nigel the gnome about to eat his breakfast)

I CAN . . .

Funny face 2- -

1	Read my writing and edit it to make sense.	
2	Sometimes use full stops and CAPITAL letters for sentences.	
3	Stop putting capital letters in the middle of words.	
4	Spell words I know correctly.	
5	Find small words inside big ones to help me be a better speller.	
6	Make letters start and stop in the right place.	
7	Use interesting words in my writing.	
8	Use **and** to make a sentence longer.	

I CAN . . .

2 children   -2-

1	Use l o n g + short sentences.	
2	Use **but** to make a sentence longer.	
3	Know which tense I am working in.	
4	Use interesting words to describe people, places and events.	
5	Usually put full stops and CAPITAL letters in the right place.	
6	(a) Use exclamation marks **!** (b) Use commas **,** in lists.	
7	(a) Use sounds to spell correctly. (b) Use letter patterns to spell correctly.	
8	Write **g** sitting on the line. Write **p** sitting on the line. Write **j** sitting on the line. Write **q** sitting on the line. Write **y** sitting on the line.	
9	Write **t** taller than other letters. Write **l** taller than other letters. Write **k** taller than other letters. Write **f** taller than other letters. Write **b** taller than other letters. Write **d** taller than other letters.	
10	Write several sentences about the same thing.	
Edit	**Make sure CAPITAL letters are in the proper place.**	
	Put in some really good adjectives.	

I CAN . . .

Penguin on holiday

- -2

1	Use good adjectives.	
2	Join sentences with the word **but**. Join sentences with the word **and**. Join sentences with the word **then**.	
3	Write every sentence using a CAPITAL letter and full stop.	
4	Use adverbs (e.g. slowly, silently, carefully).	
5	(a) use exclamation marks **!** in the right place. (b) use commas **,** in the right place.	
6	Make sure others can read my writing.	
7	Use technical words (so instead of "dog," say what sort of dog).	
8	Start sentences with different words.	
9	Write a good opening sentence.	
10	Tell the reader what I think.	
11	Write for an audience.	
Edit	**Reread my work to see if it makes sense.**	
	Check that every sentence has a capital letter and full stop.	
	Find the word "and" – see if I can take it out.	
	Check spellings.	

© Heather Butler 2010 *Literacy in Action: Football* Routledge

I CAN . . .

Trainer   **3- -**

1	Put " " round what people say.	
2	Join sentences with the word **because**. Join sentences with the word **as**. Join sentences with the word **then**. Join sentences with the word **so**.	
3	Make the first words in sentences different.	
4	Use **?**	
5	Join up some of my letters correctly.	
6	Take something I have read about and use it in my writing (like a character from a book or non-fiction research).	
7	Write a paragraph.	
8	Use the right tense when writing a verb (most of the time).	
9	Write a list with commas between each word.	
10	Split words into syllables to help my spelling.	
11	Spot word families (e.g. light, right, fight, might).	
12	Use headings to organise information.	
13	Write in a sensible order.	
Edit	**Change words to make something clearer.**	
	Make sure I have put in full stops.	
	Make sure question marks are after questions.	
	Make sure all capital letters are in the right place.	
	Change the words then, and or but if they are at the beginning of a sentence.	

I CAN . . .

Twirly flower

1	Use adverbs (slowly, cautiously).	
2	Use **although** as a connective.	
3	Use exclamation marks **!** properly.	
4	Put a **,** before the **"** when some one has been speaking – *"Hello,**" said Fred.*	
5	Include one simile. Include one metaphor.	
6	Write two paragraphs.	
7	Show that I know different spellings for words that sound the same (to, two, too/there, their, they're).	
8	Join all my letters correctly.	
9	Use an idea I have read and recycled as mine.	
10	(a) Take time to make sure capital letters are in the right place. (b) Take time to make sure full stops are in the right place. (c) Take time to make sure question marks are in the right place.	
11	Use small words I do know to help me spell harder words.	
12	Organise information under headings and in a sensible order.	
13	Make sure my writing has an opening and closing sentence.	
Edit	**Add some details to make your writing more interesting.**	
	Add a connective to join two sentences.	
	Correct three spellings (use a dictionary).	

I CAN . . .

A cup of tea   - -3

1	Use adverbs confidently.	
2	Use six connectives to make complicated sentences: ■ connective **and** ■ connective **but** ■ connective **as** ■ connective **then** ■ connective **so** ■ connective **because**.	
3	(a) Use speech marks " " correctly. (b) Use commas , correctly. (c) Use question marks ? correctly. (d) Use exclamation marks ! correctly.	
4	Use two similes and two metaphors.	
5	Say who my audience is and choose the appropriate style of writing.	
6	Use paragraphs most of the time.	
7	Write sentences and paragraphs that follow on from each other and make sense.	
8	Join all my letters up.	
9	Use some notes I have made after reading.	
10	Add extra information to make my writing more interesting.	
11	Let the reader know what I think about something.	
12	Spell plural words correctly.	
13	Organise information under headings, in a sensible order.	
Edit	**Use a thesaurus to find better words.**	
	Check how to spell longer words in a dictionary.	
	Be brave enough to edit out a whole chunk of writing if it makes the story flow better.	

I CAN . . .

Man crawling out of a shark's mouth   4- -

1	Say who is going to read and enjoy what I write.	
2	Create a complex sentence by dropping in a clause to make something easier to understand.	
3	Use paragraphs.	
4	Use technical language.	
5	Complete research to add details.	
6	■ Include words with suffixes. ■ Include words with prefixes.	
7	Join my handwriting up so everyone can read what I write.	
8	Make sure everything happens in the right order.	
9	Use eight different connectives: ■ connective **before** ■ connective **after** ■ connective **as** ■ connective **then** ■ connective **so** ■ connective **although** ■ connective **because** ■ connective **however**.	
10	(a) Check that verbs are in the right tense. (b) Check that pronouns are correctly matched.	
11	Write a clear, separate introduction. Write a clear, separate conclusion or ending.	
12	Use technical language.	
Edit	**Check there are commas in lists.**	
	Check there are commas in speech.	
	Change the length of sentences.	

I CAN . . .

Tiger saying "hello"   -4-

1	Use speech so that when someone speaks the story moves on.	
2	Write directly to the reader and give my opinions about something.	
3	(a) Use brackets ( ) to add detail. (b) Use dashes –.	
4	(a) Use ! correctly without even thinking about it. (b) Use " " correctly without even thinking about it. (c) Use , correctly without even thinking about it. (d) Use ? correctly without even thinking about it.	
5	Present my work neatly.	
6	Complete research before I write.	
7	Organise my work in order.	
8	(a) Use direct speech. (b) Use reported speech.	
9	Use ten connectives correctly. **and even so as then so** **although because however if when**	
10	Use commas to separate clauses.	
11	Use prefixes and suffixes correctly.	
12	Use technical words.	
13	Write specifically for an audience.	
14	Start my writing with a really good opening sentence.	
15	End my writing with a finishing off statement or idea that links to the opening statement.	
16	Give examples to illustrate points.	
edit	Use a thesaurus to find better verbs.	
	Put in some adverbs to bring a sentence to life.	
	Improve sentences by making them longer or shorter.	
	Improve sentences by giving more information.	

I CAN . . .

A bridge with a spider scurrying across it --4

1	Use good adjectives.	
2	Use good adverbs.	
3	Use paragraphs all the way through.	
4	Make notes from books and other places as research and use them in my writing.	
5	Make sure my sentences are not too long.	
6	(a) Use sentences that have clauses dropped into them. (b) Use sentences that only have one word. (c) Use connective phrases at the beginning of some sentences.	
7	Use the right pronouns.	
8	Make sure verbs are in the correct tense.	
9	Check spellings in a dictionary.	
10	Write introductory paragraphs.	
11	Write so that my final paragraph refers back to what I have written.	
Edit	**Add quirky details to make my writing more interesting.**	
	Change words in a sentence to emphasise something.	
	Watch out for punctuation.	

I CAN . . .

Nigel the gnome about to eat his breakfast   5- -

1	Include a twist in the tail – something unexpected happens at the end of a story.	
2	(a) Use simple sentences. (b) Use compound sentences. (c) Use complex sentences.	
3	Use longer sentences for description.	
4	Use connectives to help ideas follow on from each other (alternatively, meanwhile, there again).	
5	Write a whole piece of work in the style I have chosen to write in.	
6	Be aware of the audience I am writing for.	
7	Spell accurately and check words in the dictionary.	
8	Refer to information I've read.	
9	Plan under paragraph headings in note form.	
10	Make my paragraphs link together.	
11	Use rhetorical questions to engage the reader.	
12	Make my closing paragraphs refer back to my opening one.	
13	Write from the same point of view all the time.	
Edit	**Be confident enough to remove whole chunks to make the action flow more fluently.**	
	Check speech marks.	
	Use a thesaurus to find better adjectives, verbs and adverbs.	
	Add some quirky details.	

Index